Crafting Paper Flowers

A Visual Guide to Breathtaking Botanicals

EMILY PALUSKA

stashBOOKS®

an imprint of C&T Publishing

Publisher: Amy Barrett-Daffin

Creative Director: Gailen Runge

Senior Editor: Roxane Cerda

Editor: Madison Moore

Cover/Book Designer: April Mostek

Production Coordinator: Tim Manibusan

Illustrator: Kirstie Pettersen

Photography Coordinator: Rachel Ackley

Front cover photography by Laura Metzler Photography

Lifestyle photography by Laura Metzler Photography; instructional photography by Emily Paluska, unless otherwise noted

Published by Stash Books, an imprint of C&T Publishing, Inc., P.O. Box 1456, Lafayette, CA 94549

Library of Congress Cataloging-in-Publication Data

Names: Paluska, Emily, 1986- author.

Title: Crafting paper flowers : a visual guide to breathtaking botanicals /

Emily Paluska.

Description: Lafayette, CA : Stash Books, [2024] | Summary: "Craft realistic paper flowers that stun and delight! Follow step-by-step instructions to create different plants and flowers, from zinnias and

peonies to ginkgos and ferns. Each flower is broken down into individual pieces, making the projects accessible to all craft levels. Combine these projects for stunning arrangements, garlands, and more"-- Provided by publisher.

Identifiers: LCCN 2023058902 | ISBN 9781644034675 (trade paperback) | ISBN

9781644034682 (ebook)

Subjects: LCSH: Paper flowers. | Floral decorations. | BISAC: CRAFTS & HOBBIES / Papercrafts | CRAFTS & HOBBIES / General

Classification: LCC TT892 .P36 2024 | DDC 745.92--dc23/eng/20240129

LC record available at https://lccn.loc.gov/2023058902

Printed in China

10 9 8 7 6 5 4 3 2 1

Dedication

For 하준 and 화영, the two best things I've ever made.

Acknowledgments

It's hard to convey how deeply grateful I am to the following people. I'll do my best.

First, to all of the incredible people who have attended my workshops over the years: I wouldn't be here writing this book without your support. Your attendance and enthusiasm has been my inspiration. I can't thank you enough.

To my editor, Madison, who talked me off the proverbial ledge countless times while showing nonstop encouragement and support throughout the entire process.

To Laura Metzler and team for truly making this book come to life with their talent behind the lens.

To my dearest friends—Meaghan, Allison, Breana, Lauren, Kelly, Celeste, and Pei—who over the years, have encouraged me to keep moving forward whether that was with this book or life in general. I feel incredibly lucky to have so many incredible women in my life.

To my family—J, Dad, Vickie, J&J, Leslee, and Louis— for their unconditional support and love. I would be much less of a person without all of your guidance and care.

To our "bonus" family—Katherine and Carli—for keeping everything behind the scenes running smoothly while chaos reigned. I couldn't have done it without the both of you.

To the paper flower community, from which there are too many people to name, thank you for allowing me to be part of such an incredible group of artists. I feel immensely thankful to be among such massively talented and lovely people.

To my mother, who will never see this but who, if she were still alive, would be very happy to know that her book-loving daughter actually wrote one herself.

To 하준 and 화영–I'll never love anything more than I love the two of you. 사랑해.

Contents

Florals and Greenery 23

Projects...............................155

Templates............................175

About the Author...........183

Introduction

If someone had told me ten years ago that I would someday be writing a book about paper flowers, I never would have believed them.

My artistic aspirations started to flame out fairly early, when I turned in a project that I had worked really hard on, and my middle school art teacher told me, "It's okay—not everyone is good at art." The flame was fully extinguished when my Art 101 teacher, in my freshman year of college, pulled me aside the first week of class to say, "There's still time to drop the class without penalty, and I really think you should consider it." These rejections confirmed to me that some people are capable of art and some are not.

When I started making paper flowers, it wasn't because I thought I was an artist or even that I was trying to be creative. I just wanted to survive. I realize how dramatic that sounds, but in this case, it's true. At that point in my life, I had a two-year-old and a newborn baby, and I didn't know who I was anymore. Postpartum depression had made itself comfortable in my psyche during my first pregnancy and never truly left. So, after another late night of feedings and a 2 a.m. internet deep dive, I found myself ordering crepe paper after seeing some pretty floral photos on Pinterest. (An adult coloring book about a garden was also on the table, but the paper was a few dollars cheaper.)

So, that's how it started. Once the baby was asleep, I would pull out the crepe paper and try to find a tutorial online to follow. In the beginning, I made possibly the ugliest paper flowers ever created. But, grotesque or not, I was so proud of them. These flowers were physical proof that I was alive, and I existed, and I was there—proof that I needed, because at that point in my life, I felt like I was truly disappearing. I know many women before me and after me, who have, are currently having, or will experience this loneliness. If you are one of those reading now, I see you. I believe in you. Keep going. It's a terrible place to be, but the utter desperation I was feeling led me to search for a solution—which ended up being making paper flowers every night. How they looked wasn't the point. The point was that this practice became a way for me to show up for myself and keep myself accountable. It was a therapy of sorts, and over time, it started working.

Many hours of practice later, I started sharing my flowers with others online—and by "others" I mean my friend Meaghan, who would dutifully like and comment on every photo I posted. The flowers were never really meant to be seen by anyone other than close friends and family, but once I decided to share them, the audience grew. I "met" many lovely and encouraging people also making paper flowers who offered suggestions and encouragement as I kept practicing.

Over the course of time, I shared more, and eventually a store in Washington, D.C asked if I led classes. The thought of both teaching and public speaking sounded like a true nightmare to me, but I found myself sending back an enthusiastic confirmation. I'll never forget that first class. On the Uber ride there, I tried to gauge if I could get out of attending by rolling out of the car when it stopped at a stoplight. Then, when I showed up to the venue, I debated locking myself in the bathroom and not leaving until everyone else had. But, instead I made it through the three hours and left feeling a euphoria I never imagined. Those few hours made me feel alive. Watching others find joy in making flowers brought me a level of happiness and belonging I had never experienced before.

That class changed everything for me. I started teaching a few times a month all over D.C. I kept saying yes to things that I was scared of, realizing that the things pushing me out of my comfort zone were making me the happiest. I've met hundreds of incredible people in my classes from all over the world—people with different jobs, backgrounds, and lives, all of whom took a few hours from their busy lives to sit down and carve out time for themselves. I've never taken that lightly, and I never will. By picking up this book and giving it a try, you are giving yourself that same gift, and I'm grateful I get to help give you that chance.

The list of why I love sharing paper flowers is long, but one of my absolute favorite reasons is because making them does not require you to be familiar with art or crafts—or really anything. You don't need to have gone to art school or be an expert at long-studied techniques. I teach paper flowers for everyone, and that's how I think art should be taught. There is space and room for creativity for all. Art is not an exclusive club with a waiting list. Art is an open door. It has enough space at the table for everyone who would like to take a seat.

This book is for you to unwind, put your phone down, and use your hands to create. This is where you can quiet your mind and explore. Mistakes in art often lead to fabulous discoveries. You are an artist; you just might not know it yet.

Inspiration

My paper flowers are inspired by the beauty of the natural world all around us. There is surely something lovely about enjoying things that only last for a short while—like real flowers—but I have found that the everlasting beauty of paper flowers is even more special. Paper flowers are a wonderful way to recreate the stunning details and botanical anatomy of nature in a way that never fades or falls away.

When approaching how to make a paper version of a flower you're interested in, I highly encourage you to take the time to get your hands on real flowers. Dissect them. Write notes. Take photos. Understand the botany of what you're trying to recreate. The better you understand the structure of the flower, the easier it's going to be for you to see how certain elements come together.

The gingko leaf template that you will find in this book is from an actual gingko leaf that I picked up outside my children's school. I pressed it flat and dry; then I traced it to create a highly realistic leaf outline.

But, as I'm sure you know already, it's not always that easy. Getting the shapes of petals and leaves right is only part of the process. But doing a dissection will help you understand what elements make a flower look like its one-of-a-kind self. You'll discover so many nuances that you wouldn't have without firsthand experience.

You will read the word *realism* many times in this book. Often, I very much want to achieve the most realistic flower possible, but that doesn't have to be your goal. Being an artist allows for flexibility. You can both honor and respect the nature from which the flowers come while taking creative liberties.

I also want to stress that the templates, recommendations, and colors in this book are always flexible. If you find that a certain technique or method doesn't work for you, do it your own way! If you find that a flower looks best if you add ten more petals or ten fewer petals, make those changes. Follow your intuition and make your flowers uniquely your own.

Real tulips (left) and paper tulips in a new colorway (right)

Tools and Materials

Crepe Paper

The most important material used in paper flowers is crepe paper. I'm not talking about the cheap crepe-paper streamers of your youth. I use high-quality Italian paper made by Cartotecnica Rossi and German crepe paper made by Werola. These two brands will allow you to make beautiful, realistic, and long-lasting flowers in a wide variety of colors.

These papers are rarely ever sold in-person. Find Cartotecnica paper at Carte Fini (cartefini.com). Find Werola at Rose Mille (rosemille.com).

You will often hear the words *paper grain* and *paper weight*. *Paper grain* refers to the visible vertical lines made by the machines that make the paper. *Paper weight*, which varies greatly, refers to how much the paper can be stretched. The lighter the weight, the more delicate the paper is and the less stretchy it is. The higher the weight, the more durable it is and the stretchier it is. Let's break it down.

GERMAN CREPE PAPER

48-Gram Paper

This German-made crepe paper is often referred to as *extra fine* or *fine crepe*. This is the perfect paper to create delicate petals with—for poppies, peonies, and the interior of garden roses. Because it's lightweight, it can tear easily when stretched. So, it's important to be gentle when working with this paper weight.

Gloria Doublette Paper

This German-made crepe paper is most commonly called *doublette* or *dual-sided*, but it's sometimes referred to as *Gloria*. This is a 90-gram paper that is two different colors of lighter weighted paper glued together. The only exception to this is white doublette, which is white on both sides. This paper is lovely for many flowers. It holds its shape beautifully, and its barely-there paper grain makes flowers and leaves look more realistic. In this book, you will see the doublette colors written as *color 1/color 2*. These are not the official Werola names, but the names given when you buy the paper at Rose Mille.

160-Gram Paper

This paper is one of the most used in this book. The color Grass Green is almost universally perfect for leaves and stems, so you will find yourself reaching for this German paper often. It also comes in a wide range of colors and is preferred in some cases over 180-gram Italian paper because it has a less pronounced paper grain. In this book, I will again be using the color names given by Rose Mille, the distributor.

ITALIAN CREPE PAPER

90-Gram Paper

This Italian paper is a relatively new introduction in the crepe-paper world, as a wonderful alternative to German fine paper. It is more easily accessible and holds its shape well while still maintaining its delicate appearance. It has incredible stretch and barely visible machine lines, and it comes in a whole host of colors. In this book, I will use the color numbering system created by Cartotecnica.

180-Gram Paper

This is, by far, the most ubiquitous crepe paper in flower making. It's the heaviest in weight, which means it also has the most stretch. It comes in the widest color range and even in ombré and metallic colors. It does have very pronounced grain lines, but their look can be modified with various techniques. It is also the most beginner-friendly paper to work with. Its high level of stretch makes it forgiving and difficult to tear. In this book, I will use the color numbering system created by Cartotecnica.

Paints and Inks

Whether you need to mix a custom color match or add details, paints are necessary for bringing paper flowers to life.

ACRYLIC PAINT

Certain weights of crepe paper (180 gram, 160 gram, and doublette) take acrylic paint beautifully. I suggest Liquitex and Golden brands, which are a bit more expensive but high quality. An entry-level brand, like Artist's Loft at Michaels, is also excellent quality for the price.

CONCENTRATED WATERCOLORS

By far the paints I reach for the most are Dr. Ph. Martin's watercolors, specifically the Radiant Concentrated Watercolor and Hydrus lines. They can be used straight from the bottle, or mixed with water, depending on your desired saturation. These watercolors can also be mixed into acrylic paint.

ALCOHOL INK

Alcohol ink is highly concentrated pigment. To use it, thin it out by mixing a few drops with ½ cup of rubbing alcohol (either 70 percent or 90 percent). The color is very saturated, so add just a few drops at a time. If you add too much, dilute the color with more rubbing alcohol. These inks have a strong smell, so use them only in well-ventilated areas. I suggest using Tim Holtz brand inks.

ALCOHOL INK MARKERS

If you're looking to add details easily without having to go through mixing and waiting for ink to dry, alcohol ink markers are a great alternative. They are used like any other marker. They are often dual sided, with two different sized tips. Copic brand is the highest quality, but Blick Art Materials also makes a lower-cost, high quality alcohol ink marker.

SPRAY PAINT

Although spray paint is not the first coloring tool I typically reach for, it is a wonderful one to have on hand. It can be used for bulk coloring if you're low on time, and it also adds beautiful accents to solid colors of crepe. I suggest using Design Master brand.

Pastels

PanPastel is a brand of highly pigmented hard pastels. They are the highest quality, come in a large selection of colors, and can also be mixed to achieve a specific color match. As they are quite expensive, I would recommend the following colors for your starter toolbox: Bright Yellow Green, Chromium Oxide Green, Hansa Yellow, Magenta, Permanent Red, and Permanent Red Extra Dark. My favorite application tool is a dense makeup brush.

Air-Dry Clay

Air-dry clay is a beginner-friendly cure-all for making certain flower parts and accents. It dries easily overnight. My preferred brand is Crayola Model Magic.

Spun Cotton

Spun cotton shapes are perfect for flower centers and the heads of mushrooms. Smile Mercantile offers a wide variety of high-quality sizes and shapes.

Floral Wire

Floral wire comes in a variety of weights. The lower the gauge of the wire, the thinner the wire. The higher the gauge of the wire, the thicker the wire. For example, an 18-gauge wire is the thickest wire used in this book. It's often used as the main stem of a flower. Floral wire is often sold covered either in cloth or in Kraft paper, both of which are great options that are easy to work with. Bare wire is harder to work with. Paper Mart sells wire in every size and type you need.

Aquarium Tubing

Aquarium tubing, usually used in fish tanks, is the perfect way to make stems thicker and more stable. The standard size, ³⁄₁₆″, holds 18-gauge floral wire perfectly.

Adhesives

Tacky glue is the perfect glue for crepe paper. It is strong enough to hold petals in place, and it dries clear. I suggest Aleene's Original brand glue.

Hot Glue

Hot glue can add unnecessary bulk to delicate blooms, so it should be used sparingly. I use it most often to secure heavier stems like daffodil or tulip stems that require the addition of aquarium tubing. It can also be used to secure things like poppy or anemone centers securely onto the wire.

Mod Podge

Mod Podge is one of my most often used materials. It's great for adding realistic texture to leaves or buds. It can also be used to laminate two layers of crepe paper together to make handmade doublette paper. It comes in a variety of types, but I most often use matte. Gloss is also good to have on hand for certain types of leaves and petals. Less is more with Mod Podge. A light layer is all you need. Applying it with the paper grain ensures the smoothest application.

Floral Tape

Although floral tape is usually used for live floral arrangements, it can be used in paper flowers, too. It is an easy way to wrap stems. It's also very useful for making wreaths or other projects. To activate the adhesive, stretch the tape.

Curling Tools

The best curling tool, in my opinion, is a standard bead reamer. They're cheap and easy to find at any craft store. They have a nice handle and a sharp, pointed edge that allows for making detailed curves and curls. An easy household alternative would be a bamboo skewer or even a piece of thick floral wire.

Scissors

Beyond choosing the right paper, the key to great flowers is the right pair of scissors. You will experience major frustration if you aren't using high-quality scissors. By far, the best brand of scissors out there for crepe paper is Kai. They are typically used by seamstresses for cutting fabric. They come in a variety of styles. My favorite is #N5165.

I also recommend Chikamasa grape pruning shears. The blades of these scissors are slightly curved, so you're able to make intricate cuts with ease.

Floral Techniques

Color

One of my favorite things about planning a new paper flower is color matching. Although there is such a wide variety of paper colors available, sometimes you won't be able to find exactly what you need. Using paints to mix your own colors will make your flowers look even more true to life.

You don't need to go out and buy hundreds of dollars of art supplies. Start small with a few pastels, watercolors, and acrylic paints. For the most economic process, consider buying only the primary colors and mix from there. For more on coloring tools, see Tools and Materials (page 12).

PANPASTEL DIMENSION

I will instruct you to add dimension to your flowers using PanPastels in many projects in this book (for example, see Icelandic Poppies, page 82). Though you can use other brands, I highly recommend sticking with PanPastel. Sometimes you'll be instructed to add pastel color to a specific part of a flower, and sometimes you will add color generally so that a petal or leaf doesn't look too flat. In the Dahlia (page 130, pictured right), adding pink to the base of the petals completely transforms them into beautifully ombré components.

Just generally adding a layer of pastel across an entire petal or leaf instantly adds color variation and dimension to an otherwise stagnant piece of paper. As you become more comfortable with the fundamentals of paper flower making, you'll be able to easily see where pastels can be added to make your flowers even more lifelike. You'll be amazed at how the addition of a little color to just the right area can make a huge impact.

Working with Crepe Paper

STRETCHING

Oftentimes, you'll need to do something to make the paper you're working with better suit the flower you're creating. Even though many paper weights are available, sometimes there won't be a perfect option. This is when stretching the paper comes in handy. Once crepe paper stretches, it will not revert back to its original shape. So, you'll have to learn through trial and error what the perfect amount of stretch looks like.

When a project calls for stretching, physically stretch the paper out along the paper grain before you start cutting the flower shapes. As is noted in specific project instructions, sometimes you just need to slightly stretch the paper. Other times, you need to stretch it as far as it can go. Again, as you become more familiar with crepe paper and how it feels and moves, you'll be able to make the paper work for the flower you're making.

LAMINATION

I love creating my own doublette paper instead of buying it premade. This process involves laminating two pieces of paper together. Remember that doublette paper is two lightweight sheets of paper (often complementary colors) glued together to create a dual-sided, heavier-weight paper.

Tulips (page 102) are the perfect example of why I sometimes prefer handmade doublette. Tulip petals made from thin paper can't absorb the paint that's necessary for coloring them. Tulip petals made from thicker paper have too much defined paper grain. So, laminating thin paper makes perfect homemade doublette paper for this flower. Making it yourself also allows you to create custom color combinations.

To laminate your own doublette paper, choose two papers the same size. I often choose 90-gram or premade doublette paper. You can also laminate a single sheet of paper by folding it in half. Stretch the paper as far as it will stretch. Prepare your workspace with parchment paper and Mod Podge. Add a thin layer of Mod Podge to one piece of paper (or one half of the single sheet) with a foam brush, making sure to brush with the paper grain. Place the second sheet of paper directly on top of the first (or fold the single sheet), pressing them tightly together. Smooth out any air pockets or wrinkles. Let the paper fully dry.

SHAPING

Shaping petals makes them more realistic. It involves stretching them just the right amount. Crepe paper's stretch and texture will take some time and muscle memory to understand, so be patient. You'll find more specific shaping instructions in each project.

Cupping

Cupping brings a petal from 2-D to 3-D. Remember that you can always add more shape to a petal or leaf, but you cannot unstretch the paper. Start slow.

To cup a petal, hold it in the center (in both height and width) with both of your thumbs and forefingers. Then, based on the shape needed for the project, gently stretch the center of the petal away from you. The amount of stretch depends on the petal. Always focus the stretch on the interior of the petal. Do not pull and stretch the petal all the way out to the edges.

CURLING PAPER

This technique is most often used in flowers like roses where cupping and shaping isn't enough.

Hold the flower component and curling tool, like a bead reamer. Wrap the edge of the paper around the curling tool. Wrap tightly for a tighter curl or loosely for a wavier edge. Release the paper. Repeat until the desired effect is achieved.

CUTTING MULTIPLES

You'll often find it beneficial to cut multiple leaves or petals at once. There's an easy way to do this using the templates in this book.

First, set the template you need against the crepe paper. Make sure the paper grain is oriented vertically, unless otherwise noted. Cut a strip the length of the paper and wide enough to fit the template. Gently stretch the strip as needed for the project. Then set the template on top of the strip, along one edge, and accordion-fold the strip below it, making sure the folded section is large enough to fit the whole template. Fold as many times as the number of pieces you're cutting, as noted by the specific project instructions. Then cut out the template, cutting through all of the folded layers.

Assembly and Strips

Once you've completed all the elements of a flower, you need to combine them together to create a finished stem or branch. This is always done by wrapping the elements together—usually with strips of crepe paper, but sometimes with floral tape.

To attach two pieces, cut ¼" strips (see Assembly Strips, below). Dot one strip with glue. Align the wires of the two pieces you want to attach. Then, use the strip with glue to wrap the two pieces together. Wrap until the wires are secure, the connection point is smooth, and there is no visible joint. Use as many strips dotted with glue as needed.

ASSEMBLY STRIPS

Every tutorial that you'll find in this book will necessitate the use of thin strips of paper for assembly, as noted above. The strips will always be either 160-gram or 180-gram paper. The strips do not need to be perfectly uniform to work, but I suggest cutting them ¼"–½" wide for most projects. Thinner strips (¼") work better for more delicate and small components, like the florets of the Cherry Blossom Branch (page 50). For larger components, like branches or a main flower step, thicker strips (½") are more efficient.

To make these strips, cut a 12" piece of paper directly off a roll of either 160- or 180-gram paper. Fold the paper in half like a greeting card. Then, rotate the paper so the paper grain is horizontal. Using scissors, cut straight across the folded paper in strips ¼"– ½" wide.

The number of strips you need for a project will vary depending on how you wrap stems. As a base rule, I like to have about 25 assembly strips of paper on hand for each project.

Basic Leaves

Many of the flowers in this book use the same basic leaf technique.

First, cut a square of paper to the size directed by the specific project. Rotate the square so the paper grain runs vertically, then cut the square in half diagonally, making two triangles. Position the triangles so that the paper grain is now horizontal. Add a line of glue down the long side of one triangle, and then glue the two triangles together. Press down tightly to seal. **A-B**

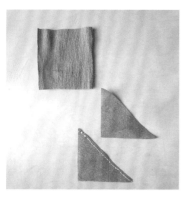

A **B**

Once dry, open the triangles. To differentiate between the top and bottom of the leaf, look at the paper grain. The grain should be extending diagonally up from the centerline. Fold the leaf closed again, and align the flat side of the required leaf template with the glued edge of the leaf. Cut the leaf shape from the triangles. Repeat to make the number of leaves directed by the project. **C-E**

C

D

E

Realism

If realism is what you're looking for, you need to include imperfections. If you look at any flower or leaf in nature, you'll see that the majority of them have nicks or divots. Nature is anything but uniform. For more on using nature as inspiration, see Inspiration (page 8).

You should always try to reference from nature. If you're working on rose leaves, try searching the web for "rose leaves macro shot." This will give you an image with a close-up look at the leaves. Use the real leaves as a road map for the paper leaves. Note the serrated edges, the variations in color from the sun or age, and any imperfections from insects or damage from weather. Then replicate these things in your process: cut serrated edges, use paint and pastels to vary leaf colors, and add holes or slits in the leaves. The littlest of details can make the largest impact.

Florals and Greenery

Each set of instructions will make one flower or branch unless otherwise noted. Be sure to review the techniques in Floral Techniques (page 16) before starting the flower and greenery projects. Find all the templates in Templates (page 175).

All templates are provided in the last section of this book, or as a downloadable PDF. To access the templates, scan this QR code, or go to tinyurl.com/11575-patterns-download.

Geranium

Geraniums are highly underrated flowers. They come in a wide variety of colors, have stunning and unique leaves, and are a symbol of good wishes and friendship.

MATERIALS

18-gauge cloth-covered floral wire

    1 piece 18″

20-gauge paper-covered floral wire

    11 pieces 5″

Doublette crepe paper in Light Rose/Pink (Werola)

180-gram Italian crepe paper in #572 (Cartotecnica Rossi)

160-gram German crepe paper in Dark Green (Werola)

Concentrated Watercolor in Raspberry (Dr. Ph. Martin's)

Copic Sketch Marker in G94

Mod Podge, matte

Foam brush

Round size 10 paintbrush

Tacky glue

Scissors

Parchment paper

Templates Needed

Templates (page 175)

    Geranium Stamen

    Geranium Petal

    Geranium Sepal

    Geranium Leaf

PAPER CUTTING

Cut Assembly Strips (page 20) of:

    Dark Green

Preparation

STAMEN

1. Use the width of the Stamen template to cut a strip of #572 the full length of the paper. Stretch the strip as far as possible. Batch cut 5 stamens (see Cutting Multiples, page 19).

2. One stamen at a time, cut a row of triangles into each stamen. Fold the strip in half, short ends together; then, angle the scissors to make pointed triangle fringe. Twist each triangular point into thinner fringe. **A-B**

3. Add a thin line of glue to the bottom edge of the stamen. Line up the top of a 5″ piece of wire with the base of the stamen. Wrap the stamen around the top of the wire, keeping the bottom edge even. Make sure the wire does not rise higher, or it will show through the middle of the flower. Press tightly. Repeat to make 5 total stamens on 5 wires. **C**

A

B

C

PETALS

1. Batch cutting 5 at a time, cut 25 petals from the Light Rose/Pink doublette (see Cutting Multiples, page 19).

2. Shake the watercolor bottle, and lay out a parchment paper work surface. Dip the round paintbrush directly into the concentrated pigment. Paint a straight line one-third of the way down from the top of 1 petal. Then fill in the bottom two-thirds of the petal below the line. The paint will bleed slightly, creating the desired petal effect. Repeat for all 25 petals. Let dry completely. **A-B**

3. Shape the petals one at a time. Hold the top of a petal with both hands, and lightly stretch the top edge in opposite directions, creating a frill. Then slightly curve the petal backward. Finally, add a small dot of glue to the backside of the petal tail, and pinch the tail closed. Repeat for all 25 petals. **C-D**

A

B

C Curving the petal

D Shaped petal

FLOWERS

1. Add a dot of glue to the front of 1 petal tail. Attach to the stamen, making the bottom of the petal even with the bottom of the stamen. Press tightly. Continue adding petals, placing 5 total in a traditional star pattern. Keep the spacing symmetrical. Repeat to make 5 flowers. **A-D**

2. Batch cut 5 sepals from the Dark Green paper (see Cutting Multiples, page 19). Curl the tops of each sepal backward. **E**

3. Add a thin line of glue at the base of the sepal. Wrap the sepal around the base of the petals, as shown. Using a Dark Green assembly strip, wrap from the base of the sepal to three-fourths of the way down the wire. Repeat for all 5 flowers. **F-G**

A

B

C

D

E

F

G

LEAVES

1. Make 6 leaves from the Dark Green paper, following the instructions in Basic Leaves (page 20). Start with 3½″ squares. Use the Geranium Leaf template. Let dry. **A**

2. Add glue to the center-back seam of each leaf and insert a 5″ piece of 20-gauge floral wire. Nestle the wire tightly to the centerline so that it's as straight as possible. Then fold the flap over and press down tightly to seal the wire inside the back of the leaf. Repeat for all 6 leaves. **B-C**

3. Set out a parchment paper work surface. Add leaf details with the Copic marker. Draw a thick circle on the bottom two-thirds of each leaf. Keep the leaves as uniform as possible. Then add a thin layer of Mod Podge to the fronts and backs of the leaves with the foam brush. Let dry. **D-E**

A

B

C

D

E

Assembly

1. Add glue to a Dark Green assembly strip. Lay the bottom 1" of a flower stem flush with the top of the 18" wire. Wrap the strip around the wires to connect them, adding more strips as needed. Wrap until smooth and secure. Attach the second and third flowers on opposite sides of the main stem at the same height as the first flower. Add the final 2 flowers on the remaining 2 sides, again at the same height, to create a symmetrical bunch of flowers at the top of the 18" wire. Wrap until secure and smooth. **A-B**

2. Using additional Dark Green assembly strips, wrap the main stem completely. Move 3" below the flowers, and lay 3 leaf stems flush with the main stem in a triangular pattern. Wrap over them until smooth and secure, and then continue wrapping 3" down the main stem. **C-D**

3. Repeat Step 2 to add the final 3 leaves in the same pattern, 3" below the first trio of leaves. Finish wrapping the whole stem. **E**

A

B

C

D

E

Zinnia

Zinnias remain one of my favorite flowers to both teach and make. They come in so many different colors and varieties, so the color options you can play with are endless. They're also deceptively simple even though they look more advanced. They're a great flower to build your flower-making confidence. They use doublette crepe paper, which has two different color sides. Remember to use the same side of the paper as directed for consistent color throughout. I am using Pink/Berry for the petals, but choose whatever color you like.

MATERIALS

18-gauge Kraft-paper-covered floral wire

> 1 piece 18″

22-gauge paper-covered floral wire

> 2 pieces 6″

Doublette crepe paper in Red/Wine, Goldenrod/Buttercup, and Pink/Berry (Werola)

160-gram German crepe paper in Grass Green (Werola)

Tacky glue

Scissors

Curling tool (bead reamer)

Bamboo skewer (with pointed tip)

Templates Needed

Templates (page 175)

> Zinnia Petal A
>
> Zinnia Petal B
>
> Zinnia Leaf

PAPER CUTTING

Cut Assembly Strips (page 20) of:

> Grass Green

Center Components

Cut:

> 14 rectangles ¼″ × 1½″ from Goldenrod/Buttercup doublette crepe paper
>
> 5 strips 1″ × 7″ from Red/Wine doublette crepe paper
>
> 1 strip ¼″ × 7″ from Red/Wine doublette crepe paper

Preparation

CENTER

1. Add dots of glue down the lighter side of the thinnest Red/Wine strip. Wrap around 1 end of the 18-gauge wire to fully cover the top 1″ of the floral wire. **A**

2. Cut a fine fringe into 3 of the 1″ × 7″ Red/Wine strips. The fringe should go two-thirds of the way down each strip and be as thin as possible. Fold each strip in half or quarters to reduce the cutting time. **B**

3. Cut thin, pointed triangles into the final 2 Red/Wine strips. The spikes should again go two-thirds of the way down each strip. Angle the scissors while cutting. **C-D**

4. Add a small line of glue along the bottom edge of 2 fringed strips. Align the paper-wrapped end of the 18-gauge wire with 1 fringed strip, aligning it below where the fringe starts. Wrap the fringe around the wire slowly, making sure to keep the bottom edge of the fringe even. Press tightly. After wrapping the first strip, add the second fringed strip, starting right where the previous fringe stopped. **E-F**

A

B

C

D

E

F

5. Trim the fringe center so it's entirely flat. Do not trim too much—you don't want to expose the wire. The center should measure about ¾″ tall. **G**

6. Use the curling tool to curl the 2 triangular strips and the final fringe strip inward. Since the dark red side should show in the final flower, make sure the light-colored side is face up as you curl. Set aside the final fringe strip. **H**

7. Add glue along the bottom edge of the 2 triangular strips. Attach 1 strip to the center, starting about ¼″ above the bottom edge of the center. The curl of the triangle fringe should hang over the trimmed fringe center. Make sure the bottom edge stays even. Add the second triangle strip where the first one ends. **I-J**

8. Cut a tiny triangle pattern into 1 short end of each Goldenrod/Buttercup strip, as shown. It should be 5 small triangles, evenly spaced. Repeat for all 14 pieces. **K**

9. Each Step 8 piece will be shaped into a star. To shape the stars, use the curling tool to curl the points of the star backward. Take note that the paper is 2 shades of yellow. The color that will show is the one that faces up as the points are curled back. Curl back the points of all 14 pieces. **L**

G

H

I

J

K

L

10. Use one unit from Step 9. Add a thin line of glue on the left edge of the golden side, stopping right below the triangle cuts. Gently fold the glued edge over to meet the other side. Then, insert the bamboo skewer into the hollow center, and press the 2 edges tightly together. With the 2 sides attached, slowly remove the skewer. Twist the bottom of the tube closed, ensuring that the hollow center of the rest of the star stays open. **M-O**

11. Repeat Step 10 for all 14 Goldenrod/Buttercup pieces. Let all stars dry completely. **P**

M

N

O

P

12. Add a thin line of glue down the bottom two-thirds of the first star tube. Attach it to the main center. The star should be slightly above the top of the red center. Repeat, adding stars around the center. The whole center will be covered by 12 to 14 stars, but you can also place fewer if you prefer. I suggest at least using 7. Press tightly on the base of each star to ensure the glue sets. **Q-S**

13. Add a line of glue along the bottom edge of the final fringed and curled Red/Wine strip. Place the strip around the stars so the inward curve of the fringe sits right underneath them. Wrap, making sure the bottom edge stays even. Press tightly. **T**

Q

R

S

T

PETALS

1. Cut 5 A petals from the Fuschia doublette paper (see Cutting Multiples, page 19). With the petals still stacked, cut a small notch in the center of the petals as shown for a natural look. Repeat to cut a total of 10 petals. **A**

2. Shape 1 petal at a time. Hold the center of a petal and gently pull with both hands. The stretch should only happen on the interior of the petal, as your thumbs and forefingers are holding the edges of the petal secure. Then curl the top part of the petal backward with the curling tool. Finally, pinch the bottom of the petal, and twist 2 or 3 times to create a tail. Repeat for all petals. **B-D**

A

B

C

D

3. Add a small dot of glue to the tails of each petal. Attach a petal to the center, slightly underneath the stars. While attaching, bend the petal back from the center at an almost 90° angle. Press tightly. Continue adding petals, making each petal just barely touch the one next to it, or leaving a tiny gap. Look from above to adjust for symmetry, and omit a petal if not all 10 are needed. **E-G**

4. Repeat Steps 1–2 with the Petal B template. Cut and shape 15 B petals instead of 10.

5. Add a small dot of glue to the tails of each Petal B. Attach a petal to the flower slightly below the first layer of petals, placing it in a gap from the first layer. Continue adding petals, filling the gaps left between the A petals by looking from the top of the flower. Add a few petals to a third layer to fill gaps if needed, and omit any petals that are not needed. **H-I**

E

F

G

H

I

LEAVES

1. Make 2 leaves, following the instructions in Basic Leaves (page 20). Start with 4″ squares. Use the Zinnia Leaf template. **A**

2. Add a thin line of glue to the center back seam of the leaf, and lay a 6″ piece of wire on top of the glue. Nestle the wire tightly to the centerline so that it's as straight as possible. Then fold over the flap and press down tightly to seal the wire inside the back of the leaf. Repeat for the second leaf. **B-C**

A

B

C

Assembly

1. Add dots of glue to a Grass Green assembly strip. Wrap the strip around the flower, starting directly under the base of the petals and then continuing until about halfway down the stem. Make sure the wrap is secure, especially at the base of the flower. Add additional assembly strips as needed. **A**

2. Halfway down the stem, lay the wire of the first leaf flush against the main stem. Then continue wrapping down, covering the leaf stem. **B**

3. Repeat Step 2, adding a second leaf on the opposite side of the stem, just below the first. **C**

4. Continue wrapping to the bottom of the stem.

A

B

C

Daffodil

When I think of spring, I think instantly of daffodils.
They are one of the first flowers to bloom, symbolizing a
new, refreshing start after the long, dark days of winter.
Most people are only familiar with the standard white and
yellow daffodils, but there are many other lovely varietals.
Some of my favorites have pink and coral elements, which
juxtapose perfectly with the cream and white petals.

MATERIALS

18-gauge cloth-covered floral wire

    1 piece 18″

20-gauge paper-
covered floral wire

    6 pieces 3¼″

180-gram Italian crepe paper in
#574 and #613 (Cartotecnica Rossi)

160-gram German crepe
paper in Grass Green and
Light Green (Werola)

90-gram Italian crepe paper
in #350 (Cartotecnica Rossi)

PanPastel in Hansa Yellow,
Orange, Bright Yellow Green,
and Chrome Oxide Green

Pastel brush

Sepia Watercolor (Dr. Ph.
Martin's Hydrus)

Mod Podge, matte

Foam brush

Aquarium tubing, ³⁄₁₆″

Tacky glue

Hot glue gun and glue sticks

Parchment paper

Curling tool (recommendation:
bead reamer)

Scissors

Templates Needed

Templates (page 175)

    Daffodil Petal A

    Daffodil Petal B

    Daffodil Corona

    Daffodil Spathe

    Daffodil Leaf

PAPER CUTTING

Cut Assembly Strips (page 20) of:

    Grass Green

    #574

Preparation

PETALS

1. Cut 2 rectangles 5″ × 10″ of #350 paper, and laminate them together (Lamination, page 18). **A**

2. Batch cut 3 Petal A petals from the Step 1 paper (see Cutting Multiples, page 19). Repeat to cut 3 Petal B petals.

3. Use the pastel brush to add Bright Yellow Green PanPastel to the bottom half of each petal. Work on a parchment paper work surface. **B**

4. Shape each petal individually. Holding the center of 1 petal with both hands, gently cup the petal. Add a dot of glue to the back tail of the petal; then pinch back the tail. Using the curling tool, curl the edges of the petal inward. Finally, use your thumb and forefinger to press defined lines and creases into the back of the petal. Repeat to shape all 6 petals. **C-D**

A

B

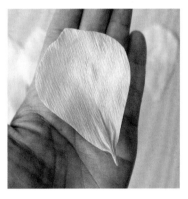

C Petal tail pinched and glued

D Edges curled and back creased

CENTERS

Each daffodil center is made up of a central stigma, pistil, five anthers, and a corona.

1. Add glue to a #574 assembly strip. Wrap the strip around the tip of the 18″ wire to create a shape like a Q-tip. **A**

2. Repeat Step 1 to wrap 5 of the 3¼″ wires. These bulbs should be slightly thinner, and the wrap should extend two-thirds of the way down the wire. **B**

3. Slightly bend the tips of each wire from Step 2. Align the 3¼″ wires around the 18″ wire, with the small anthers pointing away from the center stigma. Then, using the same #574 assembly strips, wrap the wires together. Wrap until smooth and secure, going 1″ down the stem. **C**

4. Set up a parchment paper work surface. With the pastel brush, add Bright Yellow Green PanPastel to the flower center. **D**

5. Batch cut 5 coronas using the Corona template (see Cutting Multiples, page 19).

6. On the same pastel work surface, color each corona. Color the top one-third of each corona Orange, the center one-third Hansa Yellow, and the bottom one-third Bright Yellow Green. Make the shading uniform. Use the pastel brush to blend between each color so the gradient is seamless. **E-F**

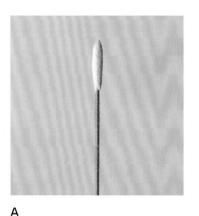

A

B

C

D

E

F

7. Tightly fold each corona into a fan shape. Pinch the bottom, and then add a small dot of glue to secure the bottom folds. Let dry completely; then open each fan, flattening and smoothing the tops of the coronas. **G-H**

8. Glue the coronas together. Add a thin line of glue down 1 edge of a corona; then press a second corona into the glue, securing them together. Repeat, attaching the coronas into a line one by one. **I-J**

9. Add a line of glue to the bottom of the corona. Wrap the corona around the center, at the base of the wrapped pistil shape. Add a final line of glue on one end of the corona to seal the corona into a ring. Press tightly to seal. Then press tightly into the pistil. Let dry completely. Once dry, open the corona. Frill the edges to add texture. **K-M**

G

H

I

J

K

L

M

SPATHE AND LEAVES

1. Cut 1 spathe with the Spathe template from the #613 paper.

2. Set up a parchment paper work surface. Use the paintbrush to paint the top seven-eighths of the spathe with Sepia watercolor. Let dry. **A-B**

3. Twist the spathe tightly, holding the bottom end flat. Set aside. **C**

4. Batch cut 3 leaves from Light Green crepe paper using the Leaf template (see Cutting Multiples, page 19).

5. On the parchment paper work surface, use the pastel brush to detail each leaf with Chromium Oxide Green PanPastel. Add multiple layers of pastel onto the majority of the leaf with only the outer edges left as their original color. **D**

6. Brush a thin layer of Mod Podge with the foam brush onto both sides of the leaves. Let dry completely. **E**

7. Hold the bottom tail of 1 leaf. Use a fingernail from your other hand to pinch the leaf between your thumb and forefinger. Run your fingers up the length of the leaf, creating a defined line down the center of the leaf. Repeat multiples times to make the crease pronounced. Repeat with the other 2 leaves. **F**

A

B

C

D

E

F

Assembly

1. Add a small dot of glue to the tails of each Petal A. Attach 1 petal to the base of the corona. Attach the other 2 Petal A petals around the corona in a triangular shape. **A-B**

2. Repeat Step 1 to add the 3 B petals in the gaps left by the A petals. Attach at the same height as the A petals. **C**

3. Run the stem into the hollow aquarium tubing to make the stem thicker. Add a small amount of hot glue to secure. Wrap Grass Green assembly strips from the base of the flower to the bottom of the stem, until it is covered completely and smoothly. **D-E**

4. Slightly bend the daffodil flower head. Align the flat end of the spathe with the stem, 2½˝ from the base of the flower. Use Grass Green assembly strips to wrap the spathe to the main stem. Wrap until it's smoothly and securely attached. **F**

5. Align the leaves in a triangular pattern around the stem, about two-thirds of the way down the stem (one-third from the bottom of the stem). Use the Grass Green assembly strips to wrap the leaves to the main stem. Wrap until the leaves are secure; then continue to the bottom of the stem for a smooth finish. **G-H**

A

B

C

D

E

F

G

H

Anemone

There are many varieties of anemones but panda anemones elicit an almost universally positive response. A black-and-white flower with an iridescent center named after arguably one of the cutest animals on the planet? What's not to like? They also add an immediate visual focal point to any arrangement. Even though they may be best known in black and white, they also come in a host of other magical colors. Part of the ranunculus family, anemones are another stunning flower to add to your repertoire.

MATERIALS

18-gauge cloth-covered floral wire
    1 piece 18″

180-gram Italian crepe paper in #600 (Cartotecnica Rossi)

160-gram German crepe paper in Grass Green and Dark Green (Cartotecnica Rossi)

90-gram Italian crepe paper in #350 (Cartotecnica Rossi)

PanPastel in Bright Yellow Green and Chrome Oxide Green

Pastel brush

Acrylic paint in Black and Interference Violet (Golden)

Paint palette or tray

Flat paintbrush

Mod Podge, matte

Foam brush

Air-dry clay (Model Magic)

Aquarium tubing, ³⁄₁₆″
    1 piece 18″

Tacky glue

Hot glue gun and glue sticks

Curling tool (recommendation: bead reamer)

Scissors

Templates Needed

Templates (page 175)
- Anemone Petal A
- Anemone Petal B
- Anemone Leaf

PAPER CUTTING

Cut Assembly Strips (page 20) of:
- Grass Green

Preparation

CENTER AND STEM

1. Break off a small piece of air-dry clay, and roll it into a ball between your palms. **A**

2. Gently press the ball onto a clean, flat surface, flattening it into a disc. It should be about ¼″ across and ¼″ thick. Stick the 18″ wire into the bottom of the clay disc so the clay is secured on top of the wire. Be careful when adding the wire so as not to accidentally poke through the disc. Let the clay dry overnight on the wire, upright. **B**

3. Prepare the paint palette with both colors of acrylic paint. Use the paintbrush to fully coat the clay center with Black paint. **C**

4. Mix a small amount of Black and Interference Violet paint, using a 2:1 ratio. Paint a second coat of this mixed color onto the center. Let fully dry. **D**

5. Secure the bottom of the center to the wire with a small bit of hot glue. Run the wire through the hollow aquarium tubing. Use more hot glue to secure the tubing directly under the base of the center. **E**

6. Cut 2 strips of #600 crepe paper 1¼″ × 9″ and stretch them out. Using the flat paintbrush, the Black paint, and the palette, paint along a 9″ edge of each strip. Paint a uniform ¼″ stripe as straight as possible. Let dry completely. Then paint a thin layer of Violet Interference paint directly over the black strip. Let dry completely again. **F**

A

B

C

D

E

F

7. Fold 1 strip into thirds. Finely fringe the painted side of the strips, cutting two-thirds of the way into the strip and cutting through all 3 layers. Make sure the fringe is as even in width as possible. Unfold. Repeat with the second strip. **G-H**

8. Add a line of glue along the long bottom edge of 1 strip. Starting with 1 short end of the strip, wrap the strip around the base of the center, fanning out the fringe as you wrap. Make sure the unfringed bottom edge of the strip remains even while the fringes extend up and out around the center. Wrap slowly and tightly until the entire first strip is wrapped. Then add glue to the second strip and continue wrapping where the first strip left off. Trim any fringes that don't look uniform in height. **I-L**

G

H

I

J

K

L

PETALS

1. Stretch a 6″ × 12″ rectangle of #350 crepe paper. Laminate the paper in half to form a 6″ square (see Lamination, page 18). Let dry. **A**

2. Batch cutting 4 at a time, cut 7 Petal A petals from the paper from Step 1 (see Cutting Multiples, page 19). Set aside the extra petal if you cut 8. From the same paper, cut 2 Petal B petals.

3. Shape the petals one at a time. Gently cup each petal by holding the center of one with both hands and gently stretching. Pinch the tail of each petal to create a defined fold. Bend the petal back 45° from the tail. **B**

4. Add glue to the tail of 1 Petal A. Attach it to the main stem, with the tail flush with the flat part of the stamen fringe. Attach a second Petal A directly across from the first petal. **C-D**

5. Attach the third Petal A next to the first petal, overlapping them as shown. **E**

6. Attach a Petal B in the small remaining gap between the second and third A petals. **F**

A

B

C

D

E

F

7. Attach a fourth Petal A in the large gap left on the flower, slightly overlapping the first petal. Start a second layer of petals. Attach them at the same height as the first layer of petals. Place the 4 remaining petals (1 Petal B, 3 Petal A) in the gaps left by the first layer. Look at the flower from the top, and place as needed, using the larger petals for larger gaps. **G-J**

8. Add glue to the Grass Green assembly strips, and use them to wrap the base of the petals, cleaning up the underside of the flower and the point where the tube connects to the flower. **K**

G

H

I

J

K

LEAVES

1. Batch cut 5 leaves in Dark Green with the Anemone Leaf Template (see Cutting Multiples, page 19). **A**

2. Lay out a parchment paper work surface. Using the pastel brush and both PanPastel colors, add color to all 5 leaves, focusing on the fingers of the leaves to add additional dimension (see Color, page 16). **B**

A

B

Assembly

1. Add more glue to the Grass Green assembly strips; then securely and smoothly wrap the entire main stem with paper.

2. Gently bend 1 leaf backward. Use the curling tool if necessary. Add a dot of glue to the tail of the leaf. Add the leaf to the stem 3½″ below the flower. **A**

3. Repeat Step 2 to add all the leaves. Place them, evenly overlapping, around the stem at the same place. Wrap the base of the leaves with the strips from Step 1 and continue wrapping to the bottom of the stem. **B**

4. Using the curling tool, curl the ends of the leaves into a variety of directions. Anemone leaves are wild, so the more variety, the better. **C-D**

A

B

C

D

MATERIALS

18-gauge Kraft-paper-covered floral wire

   1 piece 18″

   1 piece 8½″

   1 piece 5½″

20-gauge cloth-covered floral wire

   15 pieces 3″

   4 pieces 6″

180-gram Italian crepe paper in #569, #600, and #568 (Cartotecnica Rossi)

160-gram German crepe paper in Grass Green (Werola)

Turmeric (or any other orange/brown household spice)

Tacky glue

Scissors

Parchment Paper

Small tray (optional)

Templates Needed

Templates (page 175)

   Cherry Blossom Stamen

   Cherry Blossom Sepal

   Cherry Blossom Petal

   Cherry Blossom Leaf

PAPER CUTTING

Cut Assembly Strips (page 20) of:

   Grass Green

   #568

Cherry Blossom Branch

As a current resident of Washington, D.C., cherry blossoms hold a special place in my heart. Their arrival always feels like a sign of hope that the gray winter days are gone and that there are brighter and better days ahead.

Preparation

STAMENS

1. Batch cutting 5 at a time, cut 15 stamen rectangles from the #600 crepe paper (see Cutting Multiples, page 19).

2. Cut two-thirds of the way down the long side of 1 stamen, leaving the bottom one-third untouched. Cut another slit about ⅛″ away from the first slit, and continue to fringe across the entire stamen. Repeat for all 15 stamens. Twist the individual fringe. **A-B**

3. Pour a small amount of glue and turmeric into separate areas of the tray or parchment paper. Dip the tips of the fringe into the glue and then into the turmeric. Repeat for all stamens. Let dry completely. **C**

A

B

C

PETALS

1. Batch cut 5 petals from the #569 crepe paper (see Cutting Multiples, page 19).

2. With the 5 petals still stacked, gently cup the center of the petals, stretching the center. Make sure only the interior of the petal is stretched while the outside edges of the petals are untouched and retain their shape. **A**

3. Repeat Steps 1–2 until there are 15 stacks of 5 petals, totaling 75 petals.

A

LEAVES

1. Batch cut 7 leaves from the Grass Green crepe paper (see Cutting Multiples, page 19).

2. With the 7 leaves still stacked, shape the leaves just as you shaped the petals, by gently cupping the center of the leaf.

3. Repeat Steps 1–2 until there are 4 stacks of 7 leaves, totaling 28 leaves.

SEPALS, STEMS, AND BRANCHES

1. Batch cutting 5 at a time, cut 15 more stamen rectangles from the Grass Green crepe paper (see Cutting Multiples, page 19).

2. Use the Sepal Template to cut the rectangles into the sepal shape. Repeat to make 15 sepals. **A**

A

Assembly

BLOSSOMS

Each blossom is made of five petals, one stamen, and one sepal. You have prepared enough components to make 15 blossoms. Every blossom will be attached to a 3″ piece of 20-gauge cloth-covered floral wire. Repeat Steps 1–9 to create each blossom.

1. Add a thin line of tacky glue to the bottom edge of 1 stamen. Line up a 3″ piece of wire on the bottom edge of the stamen, below the fringe, so the top of the wire is not visible from the top of the stamen. Wrap the stamen around the wire tightly. Make sure there are no air pockets, and keep the bottom edge of the stamen even. Press tightly, and let dry. **A**

2. Once the stamen is dry, add a drop of glue to the bottom tail of 5 petals.

3. Line up the bottom of 1 petal with the bottom of the stamen and press together. The first 4 petals will be applied in the exact same way. **B**

4. Add the second petal to the stamen, overlapping 50% of the widest part of the first petal. **C**

A

B

C

5. Repeat Step 4 with the third and fourth petals, gradually moving around the stamen while overlapping petals.

6. For the final petal, pull the left edge of the first petal up and tuck the right edge of the final petal inside. When looking from above, the petals should look like a snail shell, each overlapping the one next to it. **D**

7. Hold at the base of the petals, and begin to open them. As you pull them open, they should look similar to a 5-pointed star. Since the glue is still tacky, adjust the positioning of the petals if needed. **E**

8. Add glue to the base of 1 sepal, and wrap it directly under the base of the petals. The pointed edge of the sepal should cup the petals. Press tightly to attach. **F**

9. Add dots of glue down a Grass Green assembly strip. Then use the strip to wrap from the base of the sepal all the way down the length of the wire, covering it entirely. Use more strips if needed. **G**

D E F G

LEAF BRANCH

Each leaf branch will be built on a 6″ piece of cloth-covered floral wire and include seven leaves. You have prepared enough components to make four leaf branches. Repeat Steps 1–5 to create each branch.

1. Add dots of glue down the center of 2 assembly strips of #568. Use them to tightly wrap an entire 6″ piece of wire, covering it completely. **A**

2. Add a dot of glue to the bottom tail of each leaf.

3. Add the first leaf to 1 end of the wire. Press tightly to secure, wrapping the bottom of the leaf around the wire. **B**

A B

4. Move down the branch roughly 1″, spacing the leaves as you prefer, and add the second leaf to the back of the branch in the same way. Then add the third leaf right on top of the second. Press tightly at the leaf base, and then open up the leaves, 1 to the right and 1 to the left of the wire. **C**

5. Repeat Step 4, moving down the branch, adding 2 more pairs of leaves, each about 1″ apart. Make sure to leave at least 2″ at the bottom of the leaf branch. **D**

C

D

BLOSSOM BRANCH

The final branch includes three blossom branches made from the 18-gauge wire.

1. Glue and wrap the 3 pieces of 18-gauge wire with the #568 assembly strips. Go over each wire 2 or 3 times to thicken the appearance of the wire. **A**

2. Hold 5 blossoms together with the top of the 18″ wire. Lay the green blossom wires flat against the brown wire. Using the same #568 assembly strips, glue and wrap the wires together. Wrap until the connection is strong and smooth. **B**

3. Repeat Step 2 with the other 2 wires, adding 3 blossoms to the 8½″ wire and 7 blossoms to the 5½″ wire. **C**

4. Adjust and position the wires so that the blooms are evenly spaced. Curve the 18″ wire to the left. The top 4″ to 5″ of the wire should be at a 90° angle. Curve the 8½″ wire to the right in the top 3″. Curve the 5½″ wire at a 90° angle in the middle, leaving the bottom 2″ straight. **D**

A

B

C

D Curve as pictured

COMPLETION

To combine all the elements, continue to glue and wrap with #568 assembly strips. Wrap tightly, and attach one component at a time.

1. Right where the wire of the 18˝ blossom branch has been curved to the left, add a leaf branch by wrapping the wires together. Make sure to wrap each component securely and smoothly before moving on to the next. **A**

2. Add the 8½˝ blossom branch wire on the other side of the first leaf branch and wrap. **B**

3. Move down the main stem 1½˝ to 2˝ below the 8½˝ branch. Add another leaf branch to the right side and wrap. **C**

4. Move down 1½˝ to 2˝. Add a third leaf branch to the other side and wrap. **D**

5. Move down ½˝. Add the final leaf branch on the right side and wrap. **E**

6. Move down 1˝. Add the final 5½˝ blossom branch to the right of the main branch and wrap. **F**

7. Wrap continuously until you reach the bottom of the 18˝ branch, making the main branch smooth and even. **G**

A   B   C   D

E   F   G

MATERIALS

18-gauge Kraft-paper-covered floral wire

    1 piece 18″

20-gauge cloth-covered floral wire

    12 pieces 3″

Doublette crepe paper in Goldenrod/Buttercup (Werola)

180-gram #568 (Cartotecnica Rossi)

Curling tool (recommendation: bead reamer)

Mod Podge, matte

Foam brush

Parchment paper

Tacky glue

Scissors

Templates Needed

Ginkgo Biloba Leaf (page 175)

PAPER CUTTING

Cut Assembly Strips (page 20) of:

    #568

    Goldenrod/Buttercup

Ginkgo Branch

The gingko tree symbolizes endurance and vitality. It can continue to grow even through the harshest conditions. Four gingko trees lived through the bombing of Hiroshima and are still alive today. Ginkgo is a visual representation of the ability to endure.

Preparation

LEAVES

1. Cut 12 strips 3″ tall from a complete fold of Goldenrod/Buttercup doublette (3″ × length of the paper). Lightly stretch the strips. **A**

2. Set out a parchment paper working surface. Pour some Mod Podge onto the paper. I am using the brighter yellow side of the paper for the outside of the leaves. Fold 1 strip in half, with the bright yellow side facing out. Then unfold it, noting the center crease. Using the foam brush, add a thin layer of Mod Podge to half of the lightly colored side. Lay a 3″ wire in the center of the strip, as shown. **B**

3. Fold the strip back in half, enclosing the wire. Press tightly, smoothing and sealing the rectangle. Repeat to make 12 wired rectangles. Let dry completely. **C**

4. Line up the Gingko Leaf template with 1 wired rectangle, lining up the tail of the leaf and the wire as evenly as possible. Cut around the template. Repeat to make 12 leaves. **D-E**

A

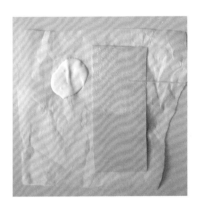

B

C

D

E

5. Add dots of glue to a Goldenrod/Buttercup assembly strip, on the light yellow side. Wrap each individual leaf, covering three quarters of each wire. **F-G**

6. Using the curling tool, curl the edges of each individual leaf toward the center front of the leaf. Don't forget to curl the bottom edges near the tail. **H-I**

F

G

H

I

Assembly

1. Add dots of glue to a #568 assembly strip. Wrap the entire 18″ Kraft-paper-covered floral wire. For a thicker branch, wrap the floral wire 2–3 times. **A**

A

2. Lay 1 leaf flush with the main stem at the top of the 18″ wire. Wrap the wires together, making sure to leave some of the yellow wire free. Wrap until they are seamlessly and tightly attached. Move down 1″ and wrap a second leaf on 1 side of the stem, bending the leaf to that side. Place the third leaf ½″ below the second leaf, on the opposite side of the stem. Wrap each leaf until secure. The added bulk from wrapping continues to make the wire look more branch-like. **B-D**

3. Place the fourth leaf ½″ below the third leaf, this time along the front/center edge of the wire. Wrap securely. Bend the leaf forward, then backward, adding a curve to the stem. **E**

4. Repeat Steps 2–3, adding leaves in the same pattern: leaf on left, leaf on right, leaf on front/center. If you prefer, add the leaves in whatever pattern you desire. After adding the final leaf, wrap to the bottom of the branch. **F**

5. Slightly bend the main branch in opposite directions along the full length for a more realistic shape. **G**

B

C

D

E

F

G

18-gauge Kraft-paper-covered floral wire

    1 piece 18″

    1 piece 7½″

    1 piece 5½″

20-gauge paper-covered floral wire

    30 pieces 3″

180-gram Italian crepe paper #613 (Cartotecnica Rossi)

160-gram German crepe paper in Grass Green (Werola)

Doublette crepe paper in White/White

PanPastel in Bright Yellow Green and Magenta

Pastel brush

Tacky glue

Scissors

Parchment paper

Templates Needed

Templates (page 175)

    Dogwood Petal

    Dogwood Small Leaf

    Dogwood Large Leaf

PAPER CUTTING

Cut Assembly Strips (page 20) of:

    Grass Green

    #613

Dogwood Branch

Dogwood trees are an indicator that a new season has arrived. Their petals are not really petals, and are technically called leaf bracts. My favorite thing about them is their durability. Their 'blooms' can last up to four weeks and add such vibrance amongst a landscape that is transitioning from the harshness of winter to the beauty of spring. This project instructs you to make the traditional white and yellow petals, but pink and yellow petals are a common variety too.

Preparation

STAMENS

1. Dot a Grass Green assembly strip with glue. Wrap the tip of 1 of the 3″ pieces with the strip, mounding the end into a Q-tip shape. To do this, wrap up and over the top of the wire a few times, and then wrap to bulk up the center. Repeat on all of the 3″ pieces to create 30 wrapped wires. Make them as uniform as possible. **A**

2. Still using Grass Green assembly strips, combine 6 of the 3″ pieces into a group. Hold 1 piece in the center; then, place 5 additional pieces around it in a symmetrical star pattern. Wrap the pieces tightly together, starting at the base of the Q-tip mounds so the centers stay in place. Repeat to make 5 separate stamen bundles. **B-C**

A

B

C

PETALS

1. Batch cutting 5 at a time, cut 20 petals from the White/White doublette (see Cutting Multiples, page 19).

2. Lay out a piece of parchment paper for a working surface. Using the pastel brush, add Magenta PanPastel to the top edge of each petal. Then add Bright Yellow Green to the bottom one-third of each petal. Make the pigment as dark or as subtle as you desire. **A-B**

3. Gently shape each petal. Hold the center of the petal with both thumbs, and gently stretch the interior part of the petal, leaving the sides intact. Pinch the bottom tail of the petal and twist. This should create a small pleat. **C**

A

B

C

LEAVES

1. Batch cutting 4 at a time, cut 8 small leaves from the Grass Green paper (see Cutting Multiples, page 19). Then, while still stacked, hold the center of the leaves with both hands, and gently cup the center of the leaves.

2. Repeat Step 1 to cut and shape 3 large leaves.

Assembly

FLOWER ASSEMBLY

1. Add a small amount of glue to the tail of each petal. Attach 1 petal to the base of 1 stamen center, bending the petal back almost 90° as you attach it. Repeat, adding a second petal directly across from the first. Add the third and fourth petals into the 2 remaining gaps. Repeat this step to create 5 flowers. **A-C**

2. Add glue to the Grass Green assembly strips, and use them to wrap each flower, starting at the base of the petals. Continue wrapping until you near the end of the wire, leaving a small piece of wire unwrapped. **D-E**

A

B

C

D

E

BRANCH ASSEMBLY

1. Add glue to the #613 assembly strips, and use them to cover the 3 pieces of 18-gauge Kraft-paper-covered floral wire. **A**

2. Using the same #613 strips, attach 1 flower to the top of each piece of 18-gauge wire. Place the wires flush against each other, and wrap until smooth, starting where the green wrapped stem stops. **B**

A

B

3. The 18″ wire is the main branch. Bend the flower on the main branch as shown. Use the same wrapping technique and strips from Step 2 to attach the 5½″ branch one-third of the way down the main branch. Wrap until secure and smooth. **C-D**

4. Add dots of glue to the tails of 3 small leaves. Attach them in a triangle pattern at the base of the 5½″ branch, where the 2 branches meet. Press tightly. Wrap the base of the leaves, and continue slightly down the branch. **E**

5. Using the same technique from Step 4, attach 2 small leaves halfway down the 7½″ branch on opposite sides. Slightly curve the branch. **F**

6. Use the same wrapping technique and strips from Step 2 to attach the 7½″ branch to the main branch, 2½″ below the 5½″ branch, on the left side. Continue wrapping down the main branch 1″ to 1½″ before adding and wrapping a stand-alone dogwood flower. **G-H**

7. At the base of the stand-alone flower, add and glue 3 small leaves in a triangular pattern around the flower. Wrap the base of the leaves, and continue slightly down the branch. **I**

8. Another 1″ to ½″ down the main branch, add and wrap the final dogwood flower. Glue the 3 large leaves in a triangular pattern below the final flower, and wrap from the base of the leaves to the bottom of the branch. Make final curve adjustments to the branch so it looks more natural. **J**

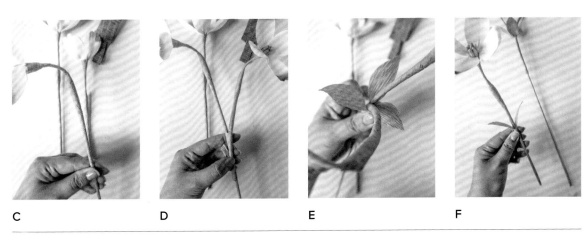

C   D   E   F

G   H   I   J

Classic Rose

A classic rose tends to be a paper flower artist's most difficult flower to learn. But, the rose is a ubiquitous flower in everyday life, and a critical flower to have in your skill set. There's a lot of trial and error, but don't be discouraged. With some practice, you'll be rewarded with a stunning, lovely flower.

MATERIALS

18-gauge Kraft-paper-covered floral wire

> 1 piece 18″

18-gauge cloth-covered floral wire

> 1 piece 8″
>
> 2 pieces 6″

20-gauge paper-covered floral wire

> 10 pieces 4″

90-gram Italian crepe paper #358 (Cartotecnica Rossi)

160-gram German crepe paper in Grass Green (Werola)

PanPastel in Permanent Red Extra Dark

Pastel brush

Tacky glue

Mod Podge, matte

Flat paintbrush

Scissors

Curling tool (recommended: bead reamer)

Parchment paper

White floral tape

Templates Needed

Templates (page 175)

> Classic Rose Petal A
>
> Classic Rose Petal B
>
> Classic Rose Petal C
>
> Classic Rose Sepal
>
> Classic Rose Leaf

PAPER CUTTING

Cut Assembly Strips (page 20) of:

> Grass Green
>
> #358

Preparation

CENTERS AND LAMINATION

1. Activate the white floral tape by stretching it. Wrap the floral tape around the top 2″ of the 18″ wire. Continue wrapping over the same 2″, making a rounded bud shape on the top of the wire. Repeat this step with the 8″ wire. **A-B**

2. Add glue to the #358 assembly strips, and then use them to wrap the pieces from Step 1. Completely cover the white "buds." **C-D**

3. Completely stretch a sheet of #358 paper. Then cut the stretched paper into 10 rectangles measuring 12″ × 8″. Laminate all 10 pieces into 6″ × 8″ rectangles (see Lamination, page 18).

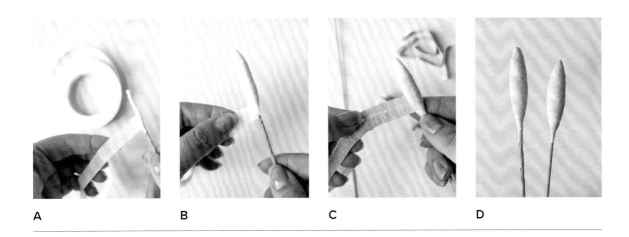

A   B   C   D

PETALS

1. Batch cut 3 petals from the laminated #358 paper using the Petal A template (see Cutting Multiples, page 19). Set aside the rest.

2. Shape each petal individually. Add nicks into the top of each petal, varying the petal edge on each one. Gently cup and stretch each petal's center. Finally, use the curling tool to curl the tops of the petals back on the top right and left sides. **A-B**

A   B

3. Put a line of glue on the left side of 1 petal, as shown. Attach it to the bud of the 18″ main stem. The top of the petal should sit ¼″ above the bud. Once the petal is secured, pull open the right side of the petal. Repeat to attach the second petal in the same way, across the bud from the first petal. Finally, add the third petal, tucking it under the second petal and overlapping it with the first petal. **C-E**

4. Glue down any remaining open points on the sides of the petals. Then curl the petal tops back away from the bud. The petals should spiral around the bud like a snail shell. **F-G**

5. Add glue to #358 assembly strips. Use the strips to wrap around the bases of the petals and create a small bulb at the base of the flower. **H**

C

D

E

F

G

H

6. Batch cut 6 petals from the homemade #358 doublette using the Petal B template (see Cutting Multiples, page 19). Repeat Step 2 to shape each petal. When curling the petal edges, make the curl as tight as possible. **I**

7. Add glue to the tail of each petal from Step 6. Place the first Petal B opposite the third Petal A on the flower. Add 2 more petals, making a triangle layer of petals. The Petal Bs should sit slightly higher than the Petal As. **J**

8. Create a second layer of 3 petals in a triangular pattern with the rest of the Petal Bs, offset from the first triangle of Petal Bs. Glue any loose petal edges down. **K-M**

9. Batch cutting 4 at a time, cut 12 petals from the laminated #358 using the Petal C template (see Cutting Multiples, page 19). Repeat Step 2 to shape each petal.

I

J

K

L

M

10. Add glue to the bottom ⅓ of the first Petal C. Place all Petal Cs slightly lower than the previous layer of Petal Bs. Glue 3 petals in a triangular pattern, again starting opposite the final Petal B. Look for gaps between the petals of the previous layer, and use the Petal Cs to fill them. Look at the flower from the top to make sure it looks symmetrical. Continue adding in groups of 3. Once you attach a set of 3, attach the next 3 petals slightly underneath the previous layer. You'll continue to follow this process until you've attached all 12 petals. **N-P**

11. Batch cut 3 petals from the laminated #358 using the Petal A template (see Cutting Multiples, page 19). Repeat Step 2 to shape each petal.

12. Repeat Steps 3–4 to attach the petals to the second bud on the 8″ stem. **Q-R**

N

O

P

Q

R

SEPALS

1. Batch cutting 5 at a time, cut 10 sepals from the Grass Green paper using the Sepal template (see Cutting Multiples, page 19). While the sepals are still stacked, cut 3 notches on each side. Gently stretch the centers of each sepal. **A**

2. Add a dot of glue on the tail of each sepal. Attach 5 sepals to the base of the bud, spaced evenly in a 5-point-star pattern. Press tightly. Curl the tops of the sepals slightly away from the bud. **B**

3. Repeat Step 2 to add the remaining 5 sepals to the underside of the main flower. Do not curl the sepals on the main flower. **C**

A

B

C

LEAVES

1. Make 10 leaves from the Grass Green paper, following the instructions in Basic Leaves (page 20). Start with 3″ squares. Use the Classic Rose Leaf template.

2. Add glue to the back seam of each leaf and insert a 4″ piece of 20-gauge floral wire. Nestle the wire tightly to the centerline so it's as straight as possible. Then fold the flap over and press down tightly to seal the wire inside the back of the leaf. Repeat for all 10 leaves. **A**

A

3. Add nicks into each leaf, following the paper grain. **B**

4. Lay out a parchment paper work surface. Using the pastel brush and PanPastel, add shading and dimension to each of the leaves (see Color, page 16). Then, using the foam brush, add a thin layer of Mod Podge to the front and back of each leaf, brushing along the paper grain. Let dry. **C-D**

B

C

D

Assembly

1. Add glue to the Grass Green assembly strips, and wrap from the base of 1 leaf to the bottom of the leaf wire. Repeat for all 10 leaves.

2. Lay 1 leaf flush against a 6″ piece of wire. Wrap both wires with the strips from Step 1, securing the wires together. Wrap until smooth. Move down 1½″ then attach 2 more leaves directly on top of one another. Wrap until smooth. Move down 1½″ more; then attach 2 more leaves directly on top of one another. Wrap until all the attachments are smooth, and continue two-thirds of the way down the wire. **A**

A

3. Open the pairs of leaves, so that they're no longer directly on top of each other. They should be tilted to opposite sides of the stem. **B**

4. Repeat Steps 2–3 to make a second leaf branch. **C**

5. Still using the Grass Green assembly strips, start wrapping around the main stem, starting at the base of the sepals. Slightly bend 1 leaf branch below the bottom pair of leaves. Then align the leaf branch with the main branch, halfway down the main branch. Wrap over the wires to attach the 2 components securely.

6. Just below the first leaf branch and on the opposite side of the main stem, align and wrap the bud to the main branch, wrapping until secure. **D**

6. Slightly bend the second leaf branch opposite the first leaf branch. Attach the second leaf branch about ½″ below the first, on the same side as the bud. Wrap until all elements are smoothly and securely attached. Continue wrapping to the bottom of the stem. Make final adjustments to the leaf and flower positioning as needed. **E**

B

C

D

E

English Garden Rose

The combinations of shapes and colors for English Garden Roses seem limitless. David Austin, a well-known and talented flower breeder, has created over 200 new rose varieties by combining garden roses with other types of roses, like floribundas and hybrid teas. This project is one of my favorite varieties.

MATERIALS

18-gauge Kraft-paper-covered floral wire

    1 piece 18˝

18-gauge cloth-covered floral wire

    2 pieces 6˝

20-gauge paper-covered floral wire

    7 pieces 3˝

    10 pieces 4˝

48-gram German extra-fine crepe paper in Blush (Werola)

180-gram Italian crepe paper in #610 (Cartotecnica Rossi)

160-gram German crepe paper in Grass Green and Dark Green (Werola)

Doublette crepe paper in Peach/Petal (Werola)

PanPastel in Bright Yellow Green and Permanent Red Extra Dark

Pastel brush

Tacky glue

Mod Podge, matte

Foam brush

Scissors

Curling tool (recommended: bead reamer)

Parchment paper

White floral tape

Templates Needed

Templates (page 175)

    English Garden Rose Petal A

    English Garden Rose Petal B

    English Garden Rose Petal C

    English Garden Rose Petal D

    English Garden Rose Petal E

    English Garden Rose Petal F

    English Garden Rose Sepal

    English Garden Rose Leaf

PAPER CUTTING

Cut Assembly Strips (page 20) of:

    Grass Green

    #610

Preparation

STAMENS

1. Cut a ¾″ × 2″ piece of #610. Cut a thin fringe into the strip, going two-thirds of the way down the rectangle. Twist the individual strips to create a textured fringe. **A-B**

2. Add glue to a #610 assembly strip. Use it to wrap the top 1″ of the 18″ piece of wire. **C**

3. Wrap the stamen from Step 1 around the top of the wire, on top of the paper from Step 2. The top of the wire should align with the base of the fringe. Wrap so that the bottom remains even, and press tightly. Trim the top of the stamen flat and even. **D-E**

A

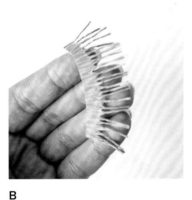

B

C

D

E

INNER PETALS

The inner petals are composed of four petal shapes (A–D), each varying in size.

1. Batch cutting 5 at a time and using the Blush paper, cut 35 petals from each of the petal templates A–D (see Cutting Multiples, page 19). This should result in 7 stacks of 5 petals for each template, or a total of 140 petals. Keep the petals stacked. **A**

2. Using the curling tool, curl the top edges of each stack of petals as much as possible. Curl the left and right sides separately. Then, using both thumbs and forefingers, gently cup and stretch the centers of the petals so the tops curl in further. Repeat for all 28 stacks of petals. **B-C**

3. Hold 1 stack of Petal D in the center. Add glue between the tails of all 5 petals. Press down, gluing the stack together at the tail. Repeat for all 28 stacks.

4. Add a dot of glue to the tail of 1 Petal D stack. Align 1 Petal C stack on top of the Petal D's, and glue them together, aligning their tails. Press tightly. Repeat this step to add on a Petal B stack and then a Petal A stack, resulting in a stack of 20 petals glued together. Keep the tails aligned. **D**

5. Add glue to the tail of 1 unit from Step 4. Add a 3″ piece of wire to the stack. Pinch the tail together, enclosing the wire. Let dry. Repeat for all stacks. **E-F**

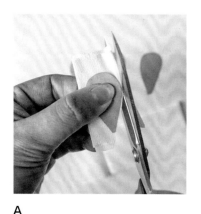

A

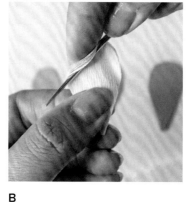

B

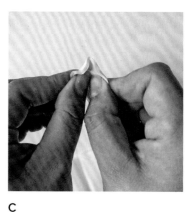

C

D

E

F

6. Activate a 6″ piece of white floral tape (use more as needed) by stretching it. Align 1 wired petal stack with the stamen on the 18″ wire. Wrap the tape around the 2 stems, securing them together. The stamen should nestle within the bottom third of the petals. **G**

7. Continue attaching each petal set around the stamen center. Work slowly to ensure that the wires are wrapped tightly together. Look at how the flower is developing from above, adjusting for symmetry. Once all the petal stacks have been added, wrap around all the wires several times to fully secure them. **H-K**

G

H

I

J

K

OUTER PETALS

Decide which side of the doublette to use as the outside of the petal. Keep this consistent throughout the project.

1. Batch cutting 5 at a time, cut 10 Petal Es (see Cutting Multiples, page 19) from the Peach/Petal doublette.

2. Shape the petals, one at a time, using your thumbs and forefingers to lightly pull the top edge of the petals in opposite directions for a ruffle effect. Make small cutouts or nicks with scissors to make realistic imperfections in each petal. Gently stretch the center of each petal, cupping them. Finally, use the curling tool to curl the top edges of the petal backward. **A-C**

3. Add a dot of glue to the tail of each petal E. One at a time, attach to the main stem, directly behind a petal stack. Petal E should align with the curve of the inner petals and sit slightly higher than the tallest inner petal. Attach the second petal, overlapping about half of the first petal. Press tightly to secure each petal. Continue adding petals in a traditional 5-point-star pattern. **D-F**

4. Repeat Step 3 to attach a second layer of petals with the remaining Petal Es. Attach them at the same height as the first layer, but between the petals of the first layer, filling in the gaps. **G-H**

A   B   C   D

E   F   G   H

5. Batch cutting 5 at a time, cut 10 Petal Fs (see Cutting Multiples, page 19).

6. Shape the petals, one at a time. Use your thumbs and forefingers to gently cup and stretch the centers of the flowers. Make small cutouts or nicks with scissors to make realistic imperfections in each petal. Finally, use the curling tool to curl the edges of the petal backward. To get a deeper curl, hold the petal around the curling tool for 5 to 10 seconds. The curls should be more pronounced than the Petal Es. **I-K**

7. Add a dot of glue to the tail of each Petal F. One at a time, attach the petals to the flower, slightly lower than the layers of Petal E. Attach a layer of 5 F petals, filling in the gaps between the previous petals. Add a second layer of 5 F petals slightly lower. **L-N**

8. Add glue to a Grass Green assembly strip. Start wrapping directly under the petal base to clean up the underside of the petals. This also acts as a way to secure your petals in place. Continue a few inches down the stem with more strips as needed. **O-P**

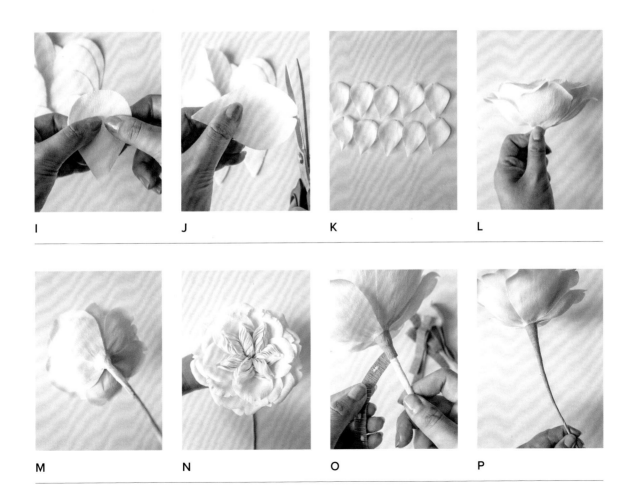

I   J   K   L

M   N   O   P

SEPAL

1. Batch cut 5 sepals from the Dark Green paper (see Cutting Multiples, page 19). Keep them stacked.

2. Cut nicks into the sepals, roughly 3 on each side, as shown. Make the nicks slightly angled. Shape the sepals, gently stretching and cupping the center of the stack. **A-B**

3. Add a dot of glue on the tail of each sepal. Attach the sepals to the main flower stem, one at a time, with the sepals curling away from the flower head. The base of the sepal should align with the base of the petals in a traditional 5-point-star pattern. **C-D**

4. Add glue to a Grass Green Assembly strip. Use the strip to wrap underneath the base of the sepals, securing and smoothing the flower base. Use more strips as needed. **E**

A

B

C

D

E

LEAVES

1. Make 10 leaves in Dark Green, following the instructions in Basic Leaves (page 20). Start with 3″ squares. Use the English Garden Rose Leaf template.

2. After cutting each leaf, add nicks to the sides, following the paper grain. **A-B**

3. Add glue to the back flap of each leaf and insert a 4″ piece of 20-gauge floral wire. Nestle the wire tightly to the centerline so it's as straight as possible. Then fold over the flap and press down tightly to seal the wire inside the back of the leaf. Repeat for all 10 leaves. **C-D**

4. Set out a parchment paper work surface. Using both colors of PanPastel, add shading and dimension to each leaf with the pastel brush, as shown (see Color, page 16). **E**

5. Then, using the foam brush, add a thin layer of Mod Podge to both the front and the back of each leaf. Apply in the same direction as the paper grain. Let dry. **F**

A

B

C

D

E

F

Final Assembly

1. Add glue to more Grass Green assembly strips. Wrap 1 leaf from the base of the leaf to the end of the wire. Repeat for all 10 leaves. **A**

2. Lay 1 leaf flush against a 6″ piece of wire. Wrap both wires with the strips from Step 1, securing the wires together. Wrap until smooth. Move down 1½″; then attach 2 more leaves directly on top of one another. Wrap until smooth. Move down 1½″ more; then attach 2 more leaves directly on top of one another. Wrap until all the attachments are smooth and secure, then continue two-thirds of the way down the wire. **B-D**

3. Spread the leaves apart, so the leaves on top of one another are positioned in opposite directions. **E**

A

B

C

D

E

4. Repeat Steps 2–3 to make a second leaf branch. **F**

5. Add glue to more Grass Green assembly strips, and start wrapping around the main stem, starting at the base of the sepals. Slightly bend 1 leaf branch below the leaves. Then align the leaf branch with the main stem, halfway down the main stem. Wrap over both of the wires to attach them securely. **G**

6. Slightly bend the second leaf branch in the other direction. Align the second leaf branch about ½˝ below the first leaf branch, on the opposite side of the main stem. Wrap to secure. Continue wrapping to the bottom of the stem. Make final adjustments to the leaf and flower positioning as needed. **H-I**

F

G

H

I

Icelandic Poppy

Icelandic poppies are one of the most adored flowers out there. With bright color combinations, ethereal crinkled petals, and curved wild stems that look like something out of a Dr. Seuss book, there's so much to love. This magical flower is a must-learn.

MATERIALS

18-gauge cloth-covered floral wire
     1 piece 18″

48-gram German fine crepe
in Vanilla (Werola)

160-gram German crepe paper
in Grass Green (Werola)

180-gram Italian crepe paper
in #566 (Cartotecnica Rossi)

PanPastel in Bright Yellow
Green and Permanent Red

Pastel brush

Acrylic paint in Titanium White
and Green Yellow (Golden)

Watercolor in Olive Green and
Chartreuse (Dr. Ph. Martin's
Radiant Concentrated Watercolor)

Paintbrush

Air-dry clay (Model Magic)

Parchment paper

Turmeric, polenta, or other
yellow/brown spice

Aquarium tubing, 3⁄16″

Tacky glue

Tray (optional)

Hot glue gun and glue sticks

Scissors

Ruler

Tweezers

PAPER CUTTING

Cut Assembly Strips (page 20) of:
     Grass Green

Preparation

CENTERS

1. Tear off a small piece of air-dry clay. Roll it in your palms to create a small gumdrop-size ball. Press into a slight cylinder. **A**

2. Use the pair of tweezers to shape a wheel spoke pattern into the top of the clay. Pinch 8 to 12 spokes. This may take multiple tries. Re-roll the clay and try again, if needed. Let dry completely overnight. **B**

3. Press the 18″ wire into the base of the clay pod. Don't poke the wire too far through the clay. Add hot glue to the wire to stabilize it to the clay. **C**

4. Thread the 18″ stem into the aquarium tubing to create a thicker stem. Hot glue the top of the tube to the base of the pod. **D**

5. Set up a parchment paper working surface and palette with Titanium White acrylic paint. Mix 3 to 4 drops of Chartreuse and Olive Green watercolor to the paint. Paint the poppy center. Let dry, and then paint a second coat. The pod should be completely green. Let dry completely, upright. **E**

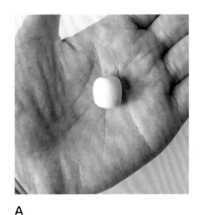

A

B

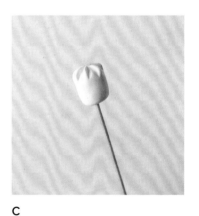

C

D

E

6. Add turmeric to the palette. Paint glue with a thin paintbrush over the "spokes" of the green center. Then dip the center into the turmeric. Let dry upright. **F-H**

7. Cut 3 pieces of #566 paper into 1⅞″ × 7″ rectangles. Stretch the paper. On the same parchment paper work surface, brush the top two-thirds of each rectangle with Bright Yellow Green PanPastel with the pastel brush. Repeat on the other side of each rectangle. **I**

8. Cut a fine fringe into each rectangle, cutting two-thirds of the way down 1 long side from the green edge. Keep the fringe as thin and uniform in width as possible. **J**

9. Dip the tip of the fringe of each rectangle into the glue and then into the turmeric. Before the glue sets, lightly separate the fringe so the pieces don't stick together. **K**

F

G

H

I

J

K

10. Add dots of glue along the bottom edge of each rectangle. One at a time, wrap each strip around the clay center. The bottom edge of the rectangles should rest on the stem just underneath the center base. The fringe should extend out from the center at a 45° to 90° angle. Wrap slowly, keeping the bottom edge even and making sure that there are no gaps in the fringe. **L-N**

L

M

N

PETALS

Each poppy is made of three small petals and two large petals. Follow the instructions to cut the petals without templates.

1. Cut 3 rectangles 3¼" × 7" and 2 rectangles 3¼' x 8"' from the Vanilla paper.

2. Fold each rectangle in half. One at a time, cut a curve into the top one-third of the rectangle. Repeat for all 5 rectangles. **A-B**

5. Set up a parchment paper work surface. Using the pastel brush, add Permanent Red to the top half of all the petals. **C**

A

B

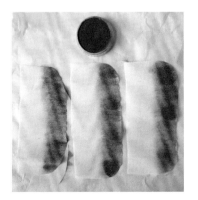

C

6. One at a time, shape each petal. Accordion-fold 1 petal by laying it flat on the work surface and then pinching the petal together along the flat edge. Hold the tail and the tip of the petal in each hand; then gently twist the petal in opposite directions. Add glue to the bottom tail; then pinch the petal back together to secure. Pinch the tail flat and then unfold the top of the petal. Finally, slightly curve the petal back at a 45 degree angle. Repeat for all 5 petals. **D-H**

D

E

F

G

H

ASSEMBLY

1. Add glue to the tail of 1 small petal; then adhere it to the main stem at the base of the fringed center. **A**

2. Add the second small petal, overlapping it with the first petal by half. **B**

3. Add the third small petal directly across from the first 2 petals. **C**

4. Add the final 2 large petals into the gaps on either side of the flower, layering the petals as shown. **D**

5. Add glue to the Grass Green assembly strips. Wrap from the base of the petals, cleaning up the underside of the flower, all the way to the bottom of the stem. Wrap as much as is needed to make the stem look smooth and stable. Add curves to the stem to mimic real poppy stems. **E-F**

A

B

C

D

E

F

MATERIALS

18-gauge cloth-covered floral wire

    1 piece 18″

    2 pieces 6″

20-gauge paper-covered floral wire

    6 pieces 3″

    6 pieces 5″

180-gram Italian crepe paper in #603 and #547 (Cartotecnica Rossi)

160-gram German crepe paper in Grass Green (Werola)

90-gram Italian crepe paper in #390 (Cartotecnica Rossi)

German doublette in Leaf/Moss (Werola)

PanPastel in Bright Yellow Green and Permanent Red Extra Dark

Pastel brush

Mod Podge, matte

Foam brush

Aquarium tubing, ³⁄₁₆″

    1 piece 18″

Tacky glue

Hot glue gun and glue sticks

Scissors

Templates Needed

Templates (page 175)

    Peony Stamen

    Peony Petal A

    Peony Petal B

    Peony Petal C

    Peony Sepal

    Peony Leaf

PAPER CUTTING

Cut Assembly Strips (page 20) of:

    Grass Green

    #603

Peony

Peonies are (nearly) universally beloved. They come in a wide breadth of colors and varieties. They are big and beautiful, and they add immediate visual impact to any bouquet or vessel they are a part of. Real peonies have a short vase life and fleeting growing season, so it's a true gift to be able to harness their magic all year round.

Preparation

CENTERS

The center of the peony is made up of six stamens.

1. Batch cut 6 stamens from stretched #547 paper (see Cutting Multiples, page 19). Add glue to the bottom two-thirds of 1 stamen. Attach the stamen to a 3″ wire by wrapping it around and pressing tightly. The top of the wire should start at the bottom two-thirds of the stamen. The top one-third of the paper should rise above the wire. Repeat for all 6 stamens. **A**

2. Add glue to #603 assembly strips, and use them to wrap around the stamen wire from Step 1, starting at the top of the wire and leaving the top of the #547 paper showing. Wrap 1¼″ down, and then add bulk in the center to create an oval-like shape. Repeat for all 6, making each as identical in size as possible. **B-C**

3. Using PanPastel in Bright Yellow Green, completely color the cream part of each stamen. Add a thin layer of Mod Podge to the entire stamen. Once the Mod Podge is dry, trim the pink paper so the stamen comes to a point. **D-F**

A

B

C

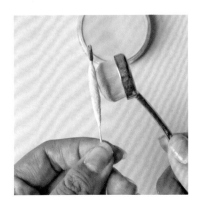

D

E

F

4. Add glue to Grass Green assembly strips. Align 1 stamen to the top of the 18″ floral wire. Wrap together with the strips, securing the stamen in place. One at a time, align the remaining 5 stamens around the first one in a traditional 5-point-star pattern, at the top of the wire. Wrap securely after adding each stamen. **G-I**

5. Add the aquarium tubing over the main stem to thicken it and help it better support the flower head. Use a small dot of hot glue to attach it securely. **J**

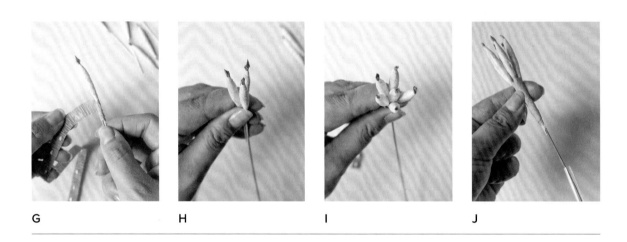

G   H   I   J

PETALS

Though you may slightly vary the number of petals on your flower, the suggested number of petals are:

- 72 Petal A
- 66 Petal B
- 10 Petal C

1. Cut the above number of Petal A and Petal B from the #547 paper in groups of 6 (see Cutting Multiples, page 19). Leave the petals in stacks.

2. Shape the Petal As in stacks. With a stack of 6 petals, use your thumbs and forefingers to gently cup the centermost part of the petals. Take care to stretch carefully—the paper is delicate in both weight and shape. Repeat for all Petal A stacks. **A**

A

3. Glue 6 petals together. Add a small amount of glue to the bottom right of the first petal; then attach at an angle as shown. Add glue over the center seam of the 2 petals; then glue a third petal on top, as shown. Repeat the placement with petals 4 through 6. First, glue petals 4 and 5 at an angle on top of the first 3 petals. Then glue the final petal in the middle of the stack. **B-E**

4. Add a small amount of glue to the base of the petal unit from Step 3, and pinch the bottom of the group of petals together to create a pleat. Slightly bend the petals back at a 45 degree angle while the glue is still tacky. **F**

5. Repeat Steps 3–4 with all the Petal A stacks to create 12 Petal A units.

6. Repeat Steps 2–4 with all the Petal B stacks to create 11 Petal B units. **G**

B Two petals

C Three petals

D Five petals

E Six petals

F

G

7. Add glue to the tail of a Petal A unit. Attach it to the stamens on the 18″ main stem. The tail of the petal should sit right underneath the base of the stamens. There is no set pattern of peony petals—the messier the better—so attach Petal A units all the way around the stamens. Once you've completed 1 layer of petals, start another layer and continue around the flower. Each new layer should be just very slightly lower than the previous layer. Press each petal unit tightly. **H-K**

8. Repeat Step 7 to add the Petal B units. Continue adding new layers, making the flower head larger and fuller. **L-M**

9. Make your own doublette by laminating 2 sheets of #390 (see Lamination, page 18).

H

I

J

K

L

M

10. Cut 10 Petal Cs from the #390 doublette. Shape the petals individually, gently cupping the center of the petal. Then use scissors to add some petal notches and variations that create a more realistic effect. **N-O**

11. Add glue to the bottom third of each Petal C, and attach them to the flower. The interior petals should sit naturally inside the Petal Cs. Arrange the first 5 petals around the flower in a traditional 5-point-star pattern. Place the final 5 petals in the gaps left by the first layer of C petals. They should be attached at the same height as the previous layer of Petal Cs. Make sure you're looking at the whole flower head from various angles to ensure you're creating an even and full shape. **P-Q**

12. Add glue to Grass Green assembly strips, and wrap the base of the petals to secure the flower and clean up the underside. **R**

N

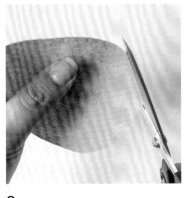

O

P

Q

R

SEPALS

1. Batch cutting 5 at a time, cut 10 sepals from the Grass Green paper (see Cutting Multiples, page 19).

2. Set up a parchment paper work surface. With the pastel brush and Permanent Red Extra Dark PanPastel, color the top edge of each sepal. **A**

3. With the foam brush, add a thin layer of Mod Podge to both sides of each sepal. Let dry completely. Gently cup the center of each sepal. **B**

4. Add glue to the bottom edge of 5 sepals. Attach them to the underside of the flower in a traditional 5-point-star pattern. The cup of the sepal should cup the flower head. Repeat to add the final 5 sepals in the gaps left by the first 5. **C-D**

5. Add glue to a Grass Green assembly strip; then wrap the base of the sepals, and continue wrapping to the bottom of the stem, covering the tubing. **E**

A

B

C

D

E

LEAVES

Remember that doublette is dual sided in color, so it's important to be consistent with which side you use for the leaves. I am using the brighter green color.

1. Make 6 leaves in Leaf/Moss, following the instructions in Basic Leaves (page 20). Start with 5″ squares. Use the Peony Leaf template. Cut a notch on the upper left and right sides of two leaves.

2. Add glue into the back seam of each leaf. Nestle a 5″ piece of floral wire into the glue, and press down tightly. The wire should be as straight as possible. **A**

A

3. On the parchment paper work surface, add Permanent Red Extra Dark PanPastel with the pastel brush across the leaf to add dimension (see Color, page 16). Add a thin layer of Mod Podge to both sides of each leaf. Let dry fully. **B-C**

4. Add glue to the Grass Green assembly strips; then wrap from the base of each leaf to the bottom of each wire. **D**

5. Combine the leaves into 2 branches. First, align 1 leaf with the top of a 6″ floral wire. Wrap the 2 wires together until smooth. Move 1½″ down the wire; then lay 2 leaves flat, on top of one another, onto the 6″ stem. Wrap the leaf wires together until smooth, and then continue down to the bottom of the wire. Open up the pair of leaves to opposite sides of the stem. Repeat to make a second branch with the other 3 leaves. **E-F**

B

C

D

E

F

Assembly

1. Align 1 leaf branch roughly halfway down the main flower stem. Attach together by wrapping with Grass Green assembly strips. Attach the second branch on the opposite side of the stem, roughly ¼″ below the first branch. Wrap to the bottom of the main stem. **A-B**

A

B

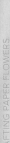
Hyacinth

Out of all the flowers in this book, I think the hyacinth is the most underappreciated. It's often used as a filler flower, though one could argue it is stunning enough on its own. When made from paper, hyacinths are time consuming since you must make many small flowers to create a finished hyacinth. The additional time and care they require is absolutely worth the effort of bringing such a beautiful flower to life.

MATERIALS

18-gauge Kraft-paper-covered floral wire
    1 piece 18″

20-gauge paper-covered floral wire
    35 to 40 pieces 3″

160-gram German crepe paper in Grass Green and Light Green (Werola)

German doublette paper in White/White (Werola)

White floral tape

Pale yellow floral stamen (World of Sugar Art)

PanPastel in Bright Yellow Green and Chrome Oxide Green

Pastel brush

Violet watercolor (Dr. Ph. Martin's Radiant Concentrated Watercolor)

Cloudy Blue alcohol ink (Tim Holtz)

70% rubbing alcohol

Measuring cups

Small plastic cups

Parchment paper

Mod Podge, matte

Foam brush

Tacky glue

Curling tool (recommendation: bead reamer)

Scissors

> NOTE • Since hyacinths require so many small flowers, buying premade artificial paper flower stamens from World of Sugar Art saves a lot of time and wire.

Templates Needed

Templates (page 175)
    Hyacinth Petal
    Hyacinth Leaf

PAPER CUTTING

Cut Assembly Strips (page 20) of:
    Grass Green
    Light Green

Preparation

PAPER

The paper for the hyacinth petals needs to be painted to achieve the signature blue-and-purple look. Work in a well-ventilated area while using alcohol ink.

1. Measure ¼ cup of rubbing alcohol. Add a squeeze of Cloudy Blue alcohol ink to the rubbing alcohol.

2. Set out a parchment paper work surface. Using the foam brush, paint an entire half fold of White/White doublette with the alcohol ink mixture. Whatever paper you don't use you can use for future hyacinths. **A**

3. In a separate cup, mix ¼ cup of water with 1 dropper of Violet watercolor. Rinse the foam brush, and then paint over the same piece of paper from Step 2. Let dry completely. **B-C**

 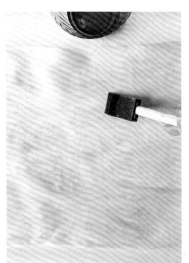 

A B C

FLOWERS

1. Batch cutting 6 at a time, cut 210 to 240 petals from the painted doublette (see Cutting Multiples, page 19).

2. To make 1 center, align 3 stamens in a triangular pattern. Slide a 3″ piece of wire into the center of the stamens, sliding it down so it's not visible from the top. Activate a piece of floral tape by stretching it; then use it to wrap the 3 stamens and wire flush together until secure. Repeat this step to make 35 to 40 centers. **A-B**

A B

3. Shape each petal from Step 1 individually. Using your thumbnail, crease a line into the center back of each petal. Repeat the crease as needed until the line is clearly defined. **C**

4. Add a dot of glue to the tail of 6 petals. Attach 1 petal to a center. The tail should sit just underneath the base of the stamen. **D**

5. To attach the rest of the petals, picture the flower like a clock. The first petal was placed at 12:00. Place the rest of the petals in the following order: 6:00, 10:00, 8:00, 2:00, 4:00. **E-I**

6. Add glue to the Grass Green assembly strips; then wrap from the base of the petals until two-thirds of the way down the wire with the strips. **J**

C

D

E

F

G

H

I

J

7. Using the curling tool, curl each petal back away from the center. If needed, repeat until the petals hold the curl. This is 1 finished flower. **K**

8. Repeat Steps 4–7 to create 35 to 40 individual flowers. **L**

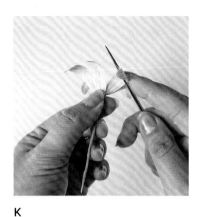

K

L

LEAVES

1. Laminate 3 Light Green rectangles 10″ × 2″, resulting in strips 10″ × 1″ (see Lamination, page 18). **A**

2. Cut a leaf from each laminated strip using the Hyacinth Leaf template.

3. On the same parchment paper work surface, use the Bright Yellow Green and Chrome Oxide Green PanPastel and pastel brush to add detail and dimension. Add darker green to the top two-thirds of each leaf and the lighter shade to the bottom one-third of each leaf. Brush a thin layer of Mod Podge to both sides of each leaf. Let dry. **B-C**

4. Use the curling tool to create a defined inward curve in the top one-third of each leaf. **D**

A

B

C

D

Flower Assembly

1. Add glue to Grass Green assembly strips. Hold 1 individual flower wire flush with the top of the 18″ wire. Wrap the 2 wires together with the strips to attach securely.

2. Slightly bend the second flower stem. Align it underneath and to the side of the first flower, along the main stem. Wrap with the same assembly strips to attach the second flower securely. **A**

3. Begin adding flowers in layers. Bend each flower wire before adding it. The flowers should be placed in layers of 5 or 6 flowers around the main stem. Wrap each individual flower securely before adding the next. The layers should be ¼″ to ½″ apart vertically on the stem. Stop adding flowers once you have reached your desired fullness. **B-D**

A

B One layer added

C Two layers added

D Four layers added

4. Continue wrapping from the final layer of flowers to the bottom of the stem. Wrap up and down the stem several times, bulking it up so it can better support the heavy flower head. **E**

E

Final Assembly

1. Add glue to the bottom one-third of each leaf. Arrange them in a triangle pattern two-thirds of the way down the main stem, attaching the leaves lower down the stem to accommodate for the flower size. Press tightly. **A-B**

2. Using Grass Green assembly strips, wrap from the base of the leaves to the bottom of the stem. **C**

A

B

C

MATERIALS

18-gauge cloth-covered floral wire
    1 piece 18″

20-gauge paper-covered floral wire
    9 pieces 2″
    6 pieces 4½″

180-gram Italian crepe paper in #602 and #603 (Cartotecnica Rossi)

160-gram German crepe paper in Grass Green (Werola)

90-gram Italian crepe paper in #350 (Cartotecnica Rossi)

PanPastel in Bright Yellow Green and Hansa Yellow

Pastel brush

Mod Podge, matte

Foam brush

Acrylic paint in Red and Light Yellow (Golden)

Paint palette or tray

Aquarium tubing, ³⁄₁₆″
    1 piece 18″

Curling tool (recommendation: bead reamer)

Tacky glue

Scissors

Hot glue gun and glue sticks

Templates Needed

Templates (page 175)
    Tulip Petal A
    Tulip Petal Covering
    Tulip Anther
    Tulip Leaf

PAPER CUTTING

Cut Assembly Strips (page 20) of:
    #603
    #602
    Grass Green

Tulip

Tulips are another prolific flower that you come across often, whether it's in the grocery store aisle or in neighbors' gardens. I think because of how often they're seen, their beauty is often taken for granted. If you ever find yourself doing that, I urge you to look at their stunning depictions in Dutch still life paintings, where their ethereal beauty is on full display.

Preparation

CENTERS

Each center is made up of three pistils and five anthers.

1. Add glue to a #603 assembly strip; then use it to wrap the tip of 1 piece of 2″ wire. Wrap to create a shape like a Q-tip on the top ¼″ of the wire. Repeat with 2 more pieces of wire. **A**

2. Bend back the wrapped tips from Step 1 so the top of all 3 wires are almost at a 90° angle. Align all 3 of the 2″ wires with the top of the 18″ wire in a triangular shape. The points should bend out from the center. Using the #603 assembly strips, glue and wrap the 4 wires together, combining them smoothly. Wrap 1¼″ down the wires, creating a slightly oval shape. **B-C**

3. Set up a parchment paper work surface. With the pastel brush and Hansa Yellow PanPastel, completely cover the pistil. Brush a thin layer of Mod Podge over the entire pistil with the foam brush. Let dry upright. **D**

4. Batch cutting 6 at a time, cut 12 anthers from #602 crepe paper (see Cutting Multiples, page 19). Brush Mod Podge onto 1 side of an anther. Place a 2″ piece of wire two-thirds of the way up the anther. Brush a second anther with Mod Podge; then use it to sandwich the wire. Press tightly to seal. If the anthers are not perfectly aligned, trim them. Repeat to make 6 total wired anthers. **E-F**

A

B

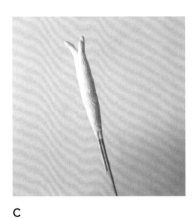

C

D

E

F

5. Add glue to the #602 assembly strips, and starting directly under the base of 1 anther, wrap to the bottom of the stem. Do not layer the wraps; keep the anther as thin as possible. Repeat to finish 5 more anthers. **G**

6. Using the foam brush, add a thin layer of Mod Podge all over all 6 anthers. **H**

7. Combine the anthers and pistil to form the center. Add glue to the Grass Green assembly strips. Align 1 anther with the base of the pistil, bending the anther out from the center at a 45° angle. The anther should be slightly higher than the pistil. Wrap the wires with the Grass Green strips to securely attach them. **I**

8. Repeat Step 7 to add all 6 anthers to the center, 1 at a time. They should be evenly spaced around the pistil. **J-K**

G

H

I

J

K

PETALS

1. Laminate 6 #350 rectangles 4″ × 8″ into 4″ squares (see Lamination, page 18). **A**

2. Follow the instructions in Basic Leaves (page 20) for all 6 squares from Step 1. Use the Petal A template to cut out each petal. **B**

3. Trim the back seam to be as small as possible. Add a line of glue on 1 side of the remaining seam, and press flat to the back of the petal. Repeat for all 6 petals. **C-D**

4. Flip 1 petal over, add a line of glue down the center, of the front side. Press a 4½″ wire into the glue. Repeat for all 6 petals. **E**

5. Completely stretch a sheet of #350. Batch cutting 6 at a time, cut out 12 Petal Coverings (see Cutting Multiples, page 19).

6. Add a layer of Mod Podge to 1 petal covering, then glue it to the front of one Petal A, sandwiching the wire. Flip the Petal A over, and repeat to add a second petal covering to the back side. Press tightly to seal. Repeat for all 6 petals. **F-G**

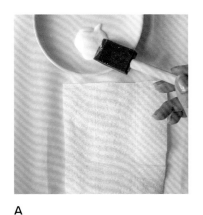

A

B

C

D

E

F

G

7. Prepare a parchment paper work surface and palette. Using the paintbrush and the Red and Light Yellow acrylic paint, add color to both sides of each petal. First, brush a feather shape over the center of the petal in Red. Then add a Light Yellow V below the feather shape. Repeat on the other side of the petal. Let dry upright. **H-I**

8. Repeat Step 8 to paint the remaining 5 petals. Make all petals as identical as possible. Let all petals dry before handling.

9. Detail the petal edges with scissors, cutting a variety of notches, rounded edges, and ruffles into the edges of all 6 petals. Cut the details following the grain of the paper. This is easiest if you turn the petal upside down. **J**

10. Use the curling tool to curl the edges of each petal inward. **K**

H **I** **J** **K**

LEAVES

1. Laminate 2 Grass Green rectangles 16″ × 2½″ into 8″ × 2½″ strips (see Lamination, page 18).

2. Cut 2 leaves from the 2 laminated rectangles from Step 1.

3. Lay out a parchment paper work surface. Using the pastel brush and PanPastel in Bright Yellow Green and Hansa Yellow, add pastel detail to both sides of the leaves, focusing the color in the centermost part of the leaves. With the foam brush, add a thin layer of Mod Podge to both sides of the leaves. Let dry. **A**

4. Curl both leaves with the curling tool. Curl the leaf tips backward, then curl the sides of the leaves inward. **B**

A **B**

Assembly

1. Add glue to Grass Green assembly strips. Align 1 petal wire with the center on the main stem. Wrap the wires together, attaching the first petal. The petal should curve inward. **A**

2. Repeat Step 1 to attach 2 more petals in a triangular pattern. The petals should all be the same height. Make sure to wrap each petal tightly before adding the next. Then, repeating the same process, add the final 3 petals, positioning them in the 3 existing gaps. Both layers of petals should be attached at the same height. **B-C**

3. Run the main stem into the hollow aquarium tubing in order to make a thick, realistic tulip stem. Add a small amount of hot glue to keep the wire and the tubing secure. Rewrap the entire stem with Grass Green assembly strips to smoothly secure the tubing. **D**

4. Add glue to the bottom one-third of both leaves, where the edges are curled inward. Align the leaves on opposite sides of the stem halfway down the length, wrapping the curled bottoms around the stem. Press securely to attach. Wrap from the base of the leaves to the bottom of the stem. **E-F**

A

B

C

E

F

D

MATERIALS

18-gauge cloth-covered floral wire
  1 piece 18″

20-gauge paper-covered floral wire
  8 pieces 5½″

26-gauge cloth-covered floral wire
  13 pieces 4″

German doublette in White/
White (Werola)

160-gram German crepe paper
in Grass Green (Werola)

180-gram Italian crepe paper in #600
and #569 (Cartotecnica Rossi)

PanPastel in Chrome Oxide Green

Pastel brush

Watercolor in Cyclamen (Dr. Ph. Martin's
Radiant Concentrated Watercolor)

Alcohol ink in Cool Peri and
Cloudy Blue (Tim Holtz)

Paintbrush

Parchment paper

Mod Podge, matte

Foam Brush

Tacky glue

Scissors

Curling tool (recommendation:
bead reamer)

Measuring cup

Small cup

Templates Needed

Templates (page 175)
  Tweedia Petal
  Tweedia Sepal
  Tweedia Small Leaf
  Tweedia Medium Leaf
  Tweedia Large Leaf

PAPER CUTTING

Cut Assembly Strips (page 20) of:
  #600
  #569
  Grass Green

Tweedia

There are not nearly enough naturally occurring blue flowers in our world. Blue is such a wonderful color to work with, and it pairs so well with other hues. If a bouquet ever feels dull, a pop of blue tweedia seems to always do the trick, changing the trajectory of your arrangement to a much more exciting place.

Preparation

FLOWERS AND SEPALS

1. Mix ¼ cup of rubbing alcohol, with a few drops of both Cool Peri and Cloudy Blue alcohol ink. Then, separately, mix ¼ cup of water with 4 or 5 drops of Cyclamen watercolor.

2. Cut a ½″ × 12″ strip of #600 paper.

3. Set up a parchment paper work surface. Paint a layer of the alcohol ink onto an entire piece of White/White doublette and the strip from Step 2. Then paint a layer of the watercolor on top of both pieces. It is not necessary to paint both sides of the paper as the alcohol ink will bleed through. Let dry completely. **A**

4. Add glue to a #600 assembly strip. Wrap the top ½″ of 1 piece of 4″ wire. **B**

5. Cut a tiny rectangle ⅜″ × ½″ from the painted #600 strip. Add glue to the bottom edge of the rectangle; then wrap it around the wire from Step 4. The top of the blue rectangle should sit slightly above the wire. Add more glue as needed to securely wrap the rectangle, but do not fold it over the tip of the wire. **C**

6. Once the glue is dry, use a pointed tool, like the bead reamer, to make sure the white wrapped wire is still visible through the blue tube. **D**

7. Repeat Steps 4–6 to create 10 total centers.

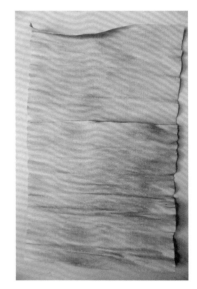

A

B

C

D

8. Five at a time, cut 50 petals from the painted doublette sheet (see Cutting Multiples, page 19). 5 at a time, cut 13 sepals from the Grass Green paper. Set aside 3 sepals for the buds.

9. Shape each petal individually. Gently cup each petal by stretching the center with both hands; then use your thumb to create a defined crease down the center of each petal. Finally, pinch the bottoms to pleat the tails. **E-F**

10. Add glue to the tail of 1 petal. Attach it to 1 wire measuring 4″ at an almost 90° angle, ⅛″ from the top of the blue tube. **G**

11. Attach 4 more petals in a 5-point-star pattern around the center. **H**

12. Repeat Steps 9–11 to create 10 total flowers. **I**

13. Using the curling tool, curl the tips of each sepal backward. **J**

14. Add a line of glue to the base of 1 sepal and wrap it around the underside of the flower. **K**

15. Add glue to Grass Green assembly strips. Wrap from the base of the sepal to the bottom of the stem.

16. Repeat Steps 14–15 to finish each flower.

E

F

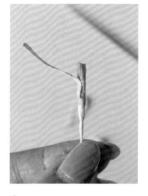
G

H

I

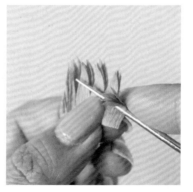
J

K

BUDS AND LEAVES

1. Add glue to #569 assembly strips. Wrap the top of a 4˝ piece of wire to create a bud shape roughly 1˝ long. First wrap the entire 1˝ section 5 to 6 times, then continue wrapping only in the center to create bulk. Repeat to create 3 buds. **A**

2. Using the foam brush, add a thin layer of Mod Podge all over each bud. Let dry upright. **B**

3. Add a line of glue to the base of 1 sepal and wrap it around the underside of 1 bud. Repeat to finish all 3 buds. **C**

4. Add glue to the Grass Green assembly strips; then wrap each bud stem from the sepal to the bottom of the stem.

5. Make 2 small leaves (start with 3˝ squares), 3 medium leaves (start with 3½˝ squares), and 3 large leaves (start with 4˝ squares) in Grass Green following the instructions in Basic Leaves (page 20). Use the 3 tweedia leaf templates.

6. Add glue to the back flap of each leaf and insert a 5½˝ piece of 20-gauge floral wire. Nestle the wire tightly to the centerline so it's as straight as possible. Then fold over the flap and press down tightly to seal the wire inside the back of the leaf. Repeat for all 8 leaves. **D**

7. Set up a parchment paper work surface. Using the pastel brush, add detail and dimension to each leaf with Chrome Oxide Green PanPastel. Then brush a thin layer of Mod Podge to both sides of each leaf with the foam brush. Let dry completely. Once dry, gently curve the leaves so the ends of the leaves are pointed downward. **E**

A

B

C

D

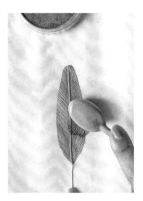

E

ASSEMBLY

1. Add glue to the Grass Green assembly strips. Wrap the top 1″ of the 18″ wire, thickening it. **A**

2. Align the 3 buds in a triangular pattern around the top of the main 18″ stem. The buds should sit just above the main stem. Wrap with the Grass Green assembly strips until they are smooth and secure. **B**

3. Align a small leaf 1½″ down the main stem, to 1 side. Wrap to secure. Then move just barely down the wire and attach a second small leaf to the other side of the stem. **C**

4. Combine 3 tweedia flowers by aligning their stems and then wrapping until they are secure. Align them at slightly different heights. Curve the stems. Repeat to make a total of 2 mini flower branches with 3 flowers each and 2 mini flower branches with 2 flowers each. **D**

5. Attach a 3-flower mini branch to the main stem 2″ below the small leaves. Attach a 2-flower mini branch just below the previous one, on the opposite side of the stem. **E**

A

B

C

D

E

6. Move 2″ down the stem, and arrange the 3 medium leaves in a triangular pattern around the main stem. Wrap to attach them. **F**

7. Move down another 1½″ on the main stem, and attach a 2-flower mini branch. Then moving down another 2″, add the final 3-flower mini branch on the opposite side of the stem. **G-H**

8. Finally, add the 3 large leaves in a slightly offset triangular pattern around the main stem, 1″ or so below the final flowers. Wrap to the bottom of the main stem. **I-J**

F

G

H

I

J

Butterfly Ranunculus

If I could dream up the perfect flower, it might look like a butterfly ranunculus. Iridescent petals? Check. Interesting color varieties? Check. Looks like something out of a fairy tale? Check. These ranunculi look absolutely otherworldly. How could they not with those glittery petals? They're perfect candidates to add a bit of movement, pop, and just the right amount of magic to an arrangement.

MATERIALS

18-gauge Kraft-paper-covered floral wire

> 1 piece 18″

> 1 piece 8″

20-gauge paper-covered floral wire

> 2 pieces 6″

180-gram Italian paper in #611 (Cartotecnica Rossi)

160-gram German crepe paper in Grass Green (Werola)

German doublette paper in White/White (Werola)

PanPastel in Bright Yellow Green, Chrome Oxide Green, and Pearlescent Red

Pastel brush

Iridescent Medium (Liquitex)

Paintbrush

Mod Podge, matte

Parchment paper

Foam brush

Tacky glue

Curling tool (recommendation: bead reamer)

Scissors

Alternate colors (optional):

> Light Yellow acrylic paint (Golden)

> Sunshine Yellow watercolor (Dr. Ph. Martin's Radiant Concentrated Watercolor)

Templates Needed

Templates (page 175)

> Butterfly Ranunculus Petal

> Butterfly Ranunculus Sepal

> Butterfly Ranunculus Small Leaf

> Butterfly Ranunculus Large Leaf

PAPER CUTTING

Cut Assembly Strips (page 20) of:

> Grass Green

Preparation

CENTERS

1. Add glue to Grass Green assembly strips, and use them to wrap the top 1″ of both the 18″ wire and the 8″ wire. **A-B**

2. Completely stretch a piece of Grass Green paper; then cut it into a ¾″ × 5½″ strip. Cut a triangle fringe into 1 long edge of the strip. Accordion-fold the strip before cutting to make the process faster. The fringe should go two-thirds of the way through the strip. Repeat to make a second triangle fringed strip. **C**

3. Completely stretch a piece of #611 paper; then cut a 1″ × 7″ strip. Cut a standard, uniform thin fringe into 1 long edge of the strip. Accordion-fold the strip before cutting to make the process faster. The fringe should go two-thirds of the way through the strip. Repeat to make a second fringed strip. **D**

4. Curl the tips of the Grass Green fringe inward. Add a thin line of glue along the bottom edge of 1 strip. Wrap the strip around the top of the 18″ wire. The base of the fringe should align with the top of the wire. Wrap carefully and tightly, keeping the bottom edge of the strip even. **E**

A

B

C

D

E

5. Repeat Step 4 to attach the second Grass Green fringe to the 8″ wire. **F**

6. Curl the tips of the #611 fringe outward. Add a thin line of glue along the bottom edge of 1 strip. Wrap the strip around the top of the 18″ wire, starting right where the Grass Green fringe ended. Wrap in the same way, keeping the bottom even and the fringe tight. When the strip has been wrapped all the way, trim the tops of the fringe to a uniform, slightly shorter height. **G-I**

7. Repeat Step 6 to attach the second #611 fringe to the 8″ wire. Trim as needed. **J**

F

G

H

I

J

PETALS

1. Batch cutting 5 at a time, cut 30 petals from the White/White doublette (see Cutting Multiples, page 19).

2. Set out a parchment paper work surface. Using the pastel brush and Pearlescent Red PanPastel, add color to the bottom two-thirds of each petal. Brush a thin layer of Iridescent Medium onto both sides of each petal. Let dry completely. **A-B**

3. Shape each petal individually. For visual interest in each flower, you want each petal to look slightly different. First, hold the tail of 1 petal and bend the rest of the petal back at a 45° angle. Crease lines with your thumb into the back of the petal, extending up from the tail and trailing in various directions up the petal. Then pinch the tail, creating a fold. Pull the top edge of the petal in opposite directions to create a ruffle. Finally, cut small nicks or imperfections into the petal with scissors. Repeat for all 30 petals. **C-F**

A

B

C

D

E

F

4. Add glue to the tail of 1 petal. Attach it to the 18˝ stem, just underneath the base of the brown fringe. Press tightly. **G**

5. Continue adding petals around the flower head by dotting the tail with glue and then pressing the petal tightly to the center. There is no set petal placement for this flower, so the more varied your placement, the better. In general, start with a layer of 5 or 6 petals around the center. Then add a second layer of petals just slightly below the first, filling in the gaps. Repeat until you've added a total of about 15 petals. **H-J**

6. Add glue to the Grass Green assembly strips. Use them to wrap from the base of the petals to the bottom of the stem. **K**

7. Repeat Steps 4–6 to create the second flower on the 8˝ stem. **L**

G

H

I

J

K

L

SEPALS, BUDS, AND LEAVES

1. Batch cutting 5 at a time, cut 10 sepals from the Grass Green paper (see Cutting Multiples, page 19). While they're still stacked, gently cup the center of the sepals by holding them with both hands and gently stretching. **A**

2. Add glue to the tail of 5 sepals. Attach them, one at a time, in a 5-point-star arrangement, around the base of the flower on the 18″ stem. **B**

3. Repeat Step 2 to attach the remaining sepals to the flower on the 8″ stem.

4. Use the Grass Green assembly strips to wrap from the base of the sepals down the entire stem, on both the 18″ and 8″ stem. Wrap until smooth. **C**

5. Using additional Grass Green assembly strips, wrap a bud shape on the ends of both 6″ wires. The buds should be 1½″ long and a bulbous oval shape. Start by wrapping the 1½″ area 5 or 6 times; then focus on wrapping only in the center to bulk up the shape. **D-E**

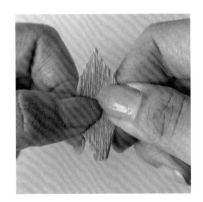

A

B

C

D

E

6. Set up a parchment paper work surface. Using the pastel brush, add Bright Yellow Green PanPastel to each bud, focusing on the top pointed section. The bud should look ombré in color. Then lightly cover each bud with Mod Podge using the foam brush. **F-G**

7. Batch cut 5 small leaves and 7 large leaves from the Grass Green paper (see Cutting Multiples, page 19).

8. On the same parchment paper work surface, add Chrome Oxide Green PanPastel to the front and back of each leaf with the pastel brush. Focus on maximizing the pigment on the centermost part of the leaves while leaving the edges their original color. Lightly cover the front and back of each leaf with Mod Podge. Let dry. **H-I**

F

G

H

I

ASSEMBLY

1. Add glue to Grass Green assembly strips. Hold the 2 buds together; then wrap the buds together tightly and securely. One bud should sit slightly higher than the other. **A**

2. Hold 3 small leaves in a triangular arrangement 1˝ below the buds. Add a dot of glue to the tail of each leaf before pressing tightly to secure. With the curling tool, gently curl the leaves outward. **B**

3. Slightly curve the 18˝ wire, just below the flower head. About 3˝ from the curve, attach 2 large leaves on opposite sides of the stem with 2 dots of glue. Press tightly. Slightly twist the ends of the leaves. Wrap from the base of the leaves to the bottom of the 18˝ stem with a Grass Green assembly strip. **C-D**

4. Another 1½˝ down the 18˝ stem, align the bud branch flush with the right side of the stem. Wrap with the Grass Green strips to attach the bud branch securely to the stem. Another 2˝ down, repeat Step 3 to add 2 more large leaves to the stem. Wrap to the bottom of the stem. **E**

5. Down the stem 1¼˝ from the Step 4 leaves, align the 8˝ stem with the second flower on the left side of the stem as shown. Lightly curve the 8˝ stem and flower head away from the 18˝ stem. Wrap the 2 stems together with the Grass Green strips until smooth and secure. **F**

6. Finally, 1˝ down from the second flower, add 3 small leaves and 2 large leaves in a 5-point-star pattern around the main stem. Attach them with a dot of glue on each tail, and press tightly. Slightly twist each leaf. Finally, wrap with Grass Green strips from the base of the leaves to the bottom of the stem. **G**

A

B

C

D

E

F

G

Ranunculus

Ranunculus remains one of the flowers that students most request to learn. It also happens to be my favorite flower—both to make and in nature. The color options are endless. They blend seamlessly in a variety of bouquets, but there's nothing quite like an entire arrangement of multicolored ranunculi to brighten the room.

MATERIALS

18-gauge Kraft-paper-covered floral wire

> 1 piece 18″

> 1 piece 6″

18-gauge cloth-covered floral wire

> 2 pieces 6″

20-gauge paper-covered floral wire

> 6 pieces 6″

160-gram German crepe paper in Light Green (Werola)

German doublette paper in Honeysuckle/Coral (Werola)

PanPastel in Bright Yellow Green and Chrome Oxide Green

Pastel brush

Mod Podge, matte

Foam brush

Air-dry clay (Model Magic)

20mm spun cotton balls (Smile Mercantile)

Curling tool (recommendation: bead reamer)

Tacky glue

Scissors

Templates Needed

Templates (page 175)

> Ranunculus Petal A

> Ranunculus Petal B

> Ranunculus Petal C

> Ranunculus Petal D

> Ranunculus Petal E

> Ranunculus Sepal

> Ranunculus Leaf

PAPER CUTTING

Cut Assembly Strips (page 20) of:

> Light Green

Preparation

CENTERS

1. Add glue to the bottom hole of a cotton ball, and then insert the tip of the 18″ piece of wire into the cotton ball. Repeat with a second cotton ball and the 6″ Kraft-paper-covered floral wire. **A-B**

2. Tear off 2 jelly-bean-size pieces of air-dry clay. Shape each piece into an oval with your palms. Place each shape on the top of each cotton ball from Step 1. Press lightly around the edges of the ovals, flattening the edges slightly and attaching the clay to the cotton. Let dry overnight. Ensure that they are propped upright so the clay can dry undisturbed. **C-E**

3. Once the clay is completely dry, use the pastel brush to completely color the clay with the Bright Yellow Green PanPastel. **F**

MAIN FLOWER

Decide which side of the doublette to use as the outside color of the ranunculus petals. Keep this consistent throughout the project. Each ranunculus uses the following petals:

- 15 Petal A
- 20 Petal B
- 25 Petal C
- 30 Petal D
- 50+ Petal E

1. Batch cut all of the petal shapes listed above from the Honeysuckle/ Coral doublette (see Cutting Multiples, page 19). Keep the petals organized and labeled so you don't mix them up.

A

B

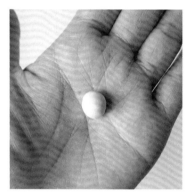

C

D

E

F

Petal A

1. Individually shape each Petal A. Cup each petal, holding the center of the petal with each hand and stretching gently. Only stretch the interior of the petal. The color that will show on the flower is the color on the exterior of the cup. **A-B**

2. Add glue to the bottom two-thirds of each Petal A. Start assembling the main flower on the 18″ stem and center. Attach 1 petal to the center, mostly overlapping the edges of the clay center. Only the top point of the clay center should show after this step. Each petal should overlap the previous petal by half. Continue adding petals around the center, pressing them tightly. Add 5 petals to make 1 complete layer. Please note that ranunculus petal placement is very specific. Take your time. Stop and look at how your flower is coming together at all different angles. **C-E**

3. Start a second layer of Petal A (5–6 petals) slightly lower than the first layer. The slight lowering of layer height needs to be subtle and incremental; otherwise, the flower will unfurl too quickly. The change in height should be almost imperceptible. **F**

4. Repeat Step 3 to add the remaining Petal As in a final layer, slightly lower than the second layer. **G**

A

B

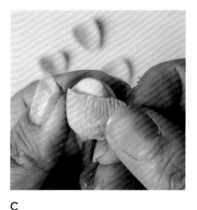

C

D

E

F

G

Petal B

1. Repeat Steps 1–4 in Petal A (left) to shape and add 20 Petal Bs to the main flower. Make sure to continue pressing each petal tightly and make each layer just slightly lower than the previous one. **A-B**

A

B

Petal C

1. Repeat Steps 1–4 in Petal A (left) to shape and add the 25 Petal Cs to the main flower. Application is the same as Petal A and Petal B, except that you will start to curve under the base of the center ball. As you're doing this, it will feel slightly unnatural. Focus on making sure that you're pressing the bases of each petal down as tightly as possible around the ball base. **A-B**

A

B

Petal D

1. Repeat Steps 1–4 in Petal A (left) to shape and add the 30 Petal Ds to the main flower. Add glue to the bottom one-third of each Petal D instead of the bottom two-thirds. This is the stage where the ranunculus will start to take shape. You may find it easier to turn the flower head upside down to add the petals to allow for more control and stability. **A-C**

A

B

C

Petal E

1. Repeat Steps 1–4 in Petal A (page 124) to shape and add the 50 Petal Es to the main flower. Add glue to the bottom one-third of each Petal E, just like with Petal D. The flower may not need all 50 petals, or you may need a few extra to complete the flower. As you add these petals, the bottom of the flower will grow wider and flatter, and the petal layers will be visible as horizontal ruffles down the side of the flower. **A-E**

A

B

C

D

E

BUD

Each ranunculus bud uses the following petals:

- 15 Petal A
- 20 Petal B

1. Batch cut the petal shapes listed above from the Honeysuckle/Coral doublette (see Cutting Multiples, page 19). Keep the petals organized and labeled so you don't mix them up.

2. Repeat the steps in Petal A and Petal B (pages 124–125) to add the petals to the 6″ stem and center. This is the completed bud.

SEPALS AND LEAVES

1. Batch cut 5 sepals from the Light Green paper (see Cutting Multiples, page 19). Curl the edges of the sepals back with the curling tool. **A**

2. Add glue to the base of 3 sepals. Wrap them underneath the base of the main flower in a triangle pattern, overlapping each sepal. **B-D**

A

B

C

D

3. Add glue to the base of the final 2 sepals. Wrap them underneath the base of the bud until it's fully covered. **E**

4. Make 6 leaves in Light Green, following the instructions in Basic Leaves (page 20). Start with 4″ squares. Use the Ranunculus Leaf template.

5. Add glue to the back flap of each leaf and insert a 6″ piece of 20-gauge wire. Nestle the wire tightly to the centerline so it's as straight as possible. Then fold over the flap and press down tightly to seal the wire inside the back of the leaf. Repeat for all 6 leaves. **F**

6. Lay out a parchment paper work surface. Using the pastel brush and both shades of green PanPastel, add color details to each leaf (see Color, page 16). **G**

7. Brush a light layer of Mod Podge onto both sides of each leaf with the foam brush. Let dry completely. **H**

E

F

G

H

Assembly

1. Add glue to the Light Green assembly strips. Align 1 leaf stem with the top of a 6″ piece of cloth-covered wire. Wrap with the glued strips, securing tightly and wrapping until smooth. Move 2″ down the 6″ stem. Lay 2 leaves directly on top of one another and flat against the 6″ stem. Wrap the second 2 leaves with the glued strips, securing them tightly and wrapping until smooth. Wrap all the way down the wire. Open up the bottom 2 leaves, bending them out to opposite sides of the stem. **A-B**

2. Repeat Step 1 to make a second leaf stem. **C**

3. Using the same Light Green assembly strips, add the bud and both leaf branches to the main flower stem. Roughly halfway down the stem, slightly bend the first leaf stem, and then align the bottom 2″ of the leaf stem wire with the main wire. Wrap to combine. Just below the first leaf stem, align and wrap the bud, attaching it. Finally, 1″ below the bud, align and wrap the second leaf stem. Continue wrapping until you reach the bottom of the stem. Slightly curve the stem. **D**

A

B

C

D

MATERIALS

18-gauge Kraft-paper-covered floral wire

    1 piece 18″

18-gauge cloth-covered floral wire

    2 pieces 6"

20-gauge paper-covered floral wire

    6 pieces 6″

German doublette in Peach/Petal (Werola)

160-gram German crepe paper in Dark Green (Werola)

PanPastel in Chrome Oxide Green, Bright Yellow Green, Magenta, and Permanent Red Extra Dark

Pastel brush

Mod Podge, matte

Foam brush

Parchment paper

Tacky glue

Scissors

Curling tool (recommendation: bead reamer)

Templates Needed

Templates (page 175)

    Dahlia Petal A

    Dahlia Petal B

    Dahlia Petal C

    Dahlia Leaf

PAPER CUTTING

Cut Assembly Strips (page 20) of:

    Dark Green

    Peach/Petal

Dahlia

Dahlias are known as the "Queen of the Garden" due to their ability to withstand harsh growing conditions. They're often the last flower standing. There are more than 40 breeds of dahlias—each one more colorful and unique than the last. Learning how to make your own paper versions permits you dahlia access any time you wish.

Preparation

CENTERS

Decide which side of the doublette paper to use as the outside color of the dahlia center. Keep this consistent throughout the project. I am using the lighter side of the paper.

1. Add glue to a Peach/Petal assembly strip. Use the strip to cover the top 1″ of the 18″ wire. **A**

2. Cut 4 strips of doublette 1″ × 10″. Cut a fine fringe into 2 of the strips. Cut two-thirds of the way down each strip and as close together as possible. Cut the other 2 strips into a fringe of rounded triangles. One triangle fringe should be slightly wider than the other. You may find it easiest to cut angular triangles first and then round them. Accordion-fold the strips before cutting for more efficient cutting. **B-C**

3. Add a thin line of glue to the bottom edge of both finely fringed strips. Align the base of 1 fringe with the wrapped tip of the 18″ wire. Wrap the strip around the wire tightly. Make sure the bottom edge of the strip remains even and pressed tightly against the stem. Add the second strip where the first one ends. **D-E**

4. Trim the fringe on the stem so it has a flat top, but do not trim low enough to expose the wire. **F**

A

B

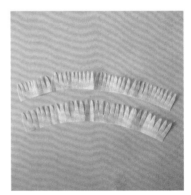

C

D

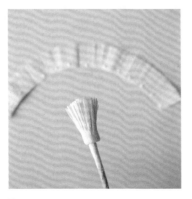

E

F

5. Set out a parchment paper work surface. Using the pastel brush, color the flat top of the fringed center with Bright Yellow Green PanPastel. **G**

6. On the same work surface, use the pastel brush to color the bottom two-thirds of both remaining fringe strips with Magenta PanPastel. Remember to color the correct side of the doublette. **H**

7. Using the curling tool, curl the edges of the fringe toward the back (white) side. **I**

8. Add glue to the bottom edge of the strip with the thinner triangles. Attach it to the center on the 18˝ stem. The base of the pink strip should sit just below where the fringe starts and hug the center. Wrap tightly, keeping the bottom edge aligned. **J-K**

9. Wrap the final strip where the previous one left off. Let the center dry for at least 1 hour. **L**

G

H

I

J

K

L

FLOWER

1. Five at a time, cut 20 each of Petal A, Petal B, and Petal C from Peach/Petal doublette (see Cutting Multiples, page 19).

2. On the parchment paper work surface, use the pastel brush to add Magenta PanPastel to the bottom two-thirds of each petal. **A**

3. Shape each Petal A individually. Hold the center of the petal with both hands and gently stretch to cup the petal. Twist the bottom of the petal (the end colored with pastel) so the edges of the petal cup inward. Repeat for all Petal As. **B**

4. Add a dot of glue to the tail of 1 Petal A. Add it to the Dahlia center. Repeat to add 10 Petal As. There is no set pattern for petal placement. Start by adding petals in the gaps left by the fringe of the center. The base of the petal should align with the base of the center. **C-E**

A

B

C

D

E

5. Add the remaining 10 Petal As in a second layer at the same height. Again, fill the gaps left by the previous layer of petals. **F**

6. Repeat Steps 3–5 with Petal B. When shaping Petal B, slightly bend back the top point of each petal after twisting the tail. Attach them at the same height as the Petal As. **G-H**

F

G

H

7. Repeat Steps 3–5 with Petal C. When shaping Petal C, create a defined pleat in the tail. You may need to crease the petal with your thumb if the twisting does not create enough of a defined line. Just as with Petal B, slightly bend back the top point of each petal. Continue to attach the petals at the same height. Depending on your preferences and the size of the flower, you may need to add more than 20 Petal Cs. Make sure the Dahlia looks symmetrical from the top, ending on a complete row. **I-K**

I

J

K

SEPALS AND LEAVES

1. Cut a rectangle 2″ × 8″ from completely stretched Dark Green paper. Accordion-fold and then cut a thick triangular fringe two-thirds of the way into the rectangle. This is the sepal. **A**

2. Use the curling tool to bend the top of each triangle back. **B**

A

B

3. Add a line of glue to the bottom edge of the sepal. Wrap it under the base of the dahlia. **C-D**

4. Use the Dark Green assembly strips to wrap from the base of the stamen to the bottom of the 18″ stem. **E**

5. Make 6 leaves from Dark Green paper, following the instructions in Basic Leaves (page 20). Use the Dahlia Leaf template. Start with 4½″ squares. Cut small notches in all the leaves.

6. Add glue to the back seam of each leaf and insert a 6″ piece of 20-gauge wire. Nestle the wire tightly to the centerline so it's as straight as possible. Then fold over the flap and press down tightly to seal the wire inside the back of the leaf. Repeat for all 6 leaves. **F**

C

D

E

F

7. Add glue to the Dark Green assembly strips. Align 1 leaf stem with the top of a 6″ piece of cloth-covered wire. Wrap together with the strips, securing tightly and smoothly. Move 2″ down the 6″ stem. Lay 2 leaves directly on top of one another and flat against the 6″ stem. Wrap with the glued strips, securing them tightly and wrapping until smooth. Wrap all the way down the wire. Open up the bottom 2 leaves, bending them out to opposite sides of the stem. Repeat with the other 3 leaves and remaining 6″ wire.

8. Slightly curve the flower head. Using more Dark Green assembly strips, wrap from the base of the sepals to the middle of the main stem. Slightly bend the first leaf branch and align to one side of the stem. Wrap until secure. Move slightly down and add the second leaf branch on the opposite side. Continue wrapping to the bottom of the stem. **G-H**

G H

MATERIALS

18-gauge cloth-covered floral wire

1 piece 18″

German doublette paper
in Leaf/Moss (Werola)

160-gram German crepe paper
in Grass Green (Werola)

Tacky glue

Mod Podge, matte

Foam brush

Scissors

Parchment paper

Templates Needed

Ruscus Leaf Template (page 175)

PAPER CUTTING

Cut Assembly Strips (page 20) of:

    Grass Green

Classic Ruscus

Ruscus greenery is the best of both worlds. It's perfect to add elegance to any bouquet, or beautiful on its own in a vase. There are many different varieties of ruscus, but this one is my favorite. Perhaps it will be yours too.

Preparation

LEAVES

Each ruscus stem uses 16 leaves. Choose which side of the doublette paper will be the front of the leaves. I'm using the brighter color.

1. Batch cutting 4 at a time, cut 16 leaves from the Leaf/Moss doublette paper using the template (see Cutting Multiples, page 19).

2. Lay out a parchment paper work surface. Using the foam brush, add a thin layer of Mod Podge to both sides of each leaf. Let dry. **A**

A

Assembly

1. Add glue to the Grass Green assembly strip, and then use it to completely wrap the 18″ wire. **A**

2. Shape leaves one at a time, maintaining the doublette color consistency. Hold the center of 1 leaf with both hands; then gently stretch the center, cupping the leaf. **B**

3. Add a dot of glue to the tail of 1 leaf. Attach to the top of the 18″ wire. Press firmly. **C**

A   **B**   **C**

4. Shape the next 2 leaves. Repeat Step 2 to cup 1 of the leaves normally. Cup the second leaf in the reverse, stretching the center of the leaf up. Attach the second and third leaves roughly 1″ below the top leaf, ensuring the top of both leaves faces up. Attach on opposite sides of the stem. **D**

5. Shape the next 3 leaves. Shape 1 of the leaves normally, cupping the center down. Shape the other 2 leaves in reverse, cupping the center up. Attach all 3 leaves in a triangular pattern around the stem, 1″ below the leaves from Step 4.

6. Repeat Step 4 to add 2 more leaves 1″ below the leaves from Step 5. **E**

7. Repeat Step 5 to add 3 more leaves 1″ below the leaves from Step 6. This time, cup 2 leaves normally, and cup 1 leaf in reverse. **F**

D

E

F

8. Repeat Steps 4–5 to add the final 5 leaves. The final trio of leaves should have 2 leaves cupped in reverse and 1 leaf cupped normally. **G-H**

9. Use the Grass Green assembly strips dotted with glue to wrap the stem from underneath the last trio of leaves to the bottom of the stem. **I**

G H I

Eucalyptus

Like ruscus, there are a wide variety of eucalyptus, but this particular silver dollar is my personal favorite. Both the color and the shape of the leaves really lend itself to adding the perfect je na sais quoi *to any arrangement. It is also impressive on its own in a vessel, adding a nice burst of green to any room.*

MATERIALS

18-gauge cloth-covered floral wire
    1 piece 18″

20-gauge paper-covered floral wire
    9 pieces 4½″

180-gram Italian crepe paper in #621 and #567 (Cartotecnica Rossi)

Spray paint in Herbal (Design Master)

Tacky glue

Scissors

Personal protective equipment: gloves and face mask

Parchment paper or cardboard

Templates Needed

Eucalyptus Leaf Template (page 175)

PAPER CUTTING

Cut Assembly Strips (page 20) of:
    #567

Preparation

LEAVES

Each eucalyptus stem has nine leaves.

1. Make 9 leaves from the #621 paper, following the instructions in Basic Leaves (page 20). Start with 4″ squares. Use the Eucalyptus Leaf template.

2. Add glue to the back seam of each leaf and insert a 4½″ piece of 20-gauge floral wire. Nestle the wire tightly to the centerline so it's as straight as possible. Then fold over the flap and press down tightly to seal the wire inside the back of the leaf. Repeat for all 9 leaves. **A-B**

3. Design Master spray paint should only be used outside, where there's plenty of ventilation. Follow the product instructions before using. Set up a workstation with the cardboard or parchment paper. I highly suggest using both gloves and a face mask.

4. Lay each leaf flat on the work surface. Lightly spray all the leaves with the Herbal spray paint. Let dry completely, and then flip over and spray the other side of each leaf. **C**

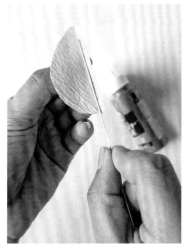

A

B

C

Assembly

1. Add glue to the #567 assembly strips, and use them to completely wrap the 18″ wire from top to bottom. **A**

2. Using the strips from Step 1, wrap each individual leaf stem, starting directly under the base of the leaf to completely cover the stem. **B**

3. Lay 1 leaf flush with the top of the 18″ wire, and then wrap tightly with glued strips from Step 1 to attach the 2 stems together. **C**

A

B

C

4. Eucalyptus leaves do not have a set growth pattern, so there is a lot of freedom in how to add each leaf. Add all 9 leaves to the stem following these basic steps:

- Bend the stem of 1 leaf, varying the stem shape.

- Lay the leaf flush against the main stem ½″ to 1″ below the previous leaf, and varying the side of the main stem.

- Wrap the leaf onto the main stem using the assembly strips of #567, wrapping until the leaf is smooth or secure. Vary the amount of the stem that is wrapped versus exposed. **D-G**

5. After adding the final leaf, wrap all the way to the bottom of the main stem.

D

E

F

G

MATERIALS

18-gauge cloth-covered floral wire

   1 piece 18″ piece

20-gauge paper-
covered floral wire

   9 pieces 6″

160-gram German crepe paper
in Grass Green (Werola)

PanPastel in Bright Yellow Green
and Chrome Oxide Green

Pastel brush

Mod Podge, matte

Foam brush

Ruler

Tacky glue

Scissors

PAPER CUTTING

Cut Assembly Strips (page 20) of:

   Grass Green

Fern

I've been fascinated by ferns ever since I saw fossilized ones from prehistoric times. It's incredible to be able to see and touch a plant that has been alive for so long. This fern can be made larger or smaller, and you can play around with the paper you use. I highly suggest trying metallic paper to create gold or silver ferns for a new spin on an old classic.

Preparation

FRONDS

There is no template for the fronds. Freehand-cut them following the instructions in this section.

1. Make 9 leaves from the Grass Green paper, following the instructions in Basic Leaves (page 20). Start with 5″ squares. Since there is no template, stop once you have the triangle pairs glued together. Orient all the leaves so the grain runs diagonally upward from the center seam. **A**

2. Mark the center point of each leaf with a ruler. Then, in both directions from the center, mark the leaves as follows:

- Mark 1 leaf 1″ from the center in both directions.

- Mark 2 leaves 1¼″ from the center in both directions.

- Mark 4 leaves 1½″ from the center in both directions.

- Mark 2 leaves 1¾″ from the center in both directions. **B-C**

3. Cut the top and bottom off of each leaf at the marks from Step 2. **D-E**

A

B

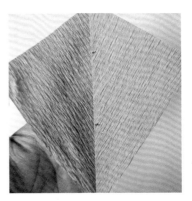

C 2″ section (1″ in each direction from the center)

D

E

4. Turn 1 leaf upside down so the paper grain is pointing diagonally down. Fold the leaf in half, matching the pointed sides. Freehand-cut the fern leaf shape. Round the top and then cut fronds into the side, working slowly. Repeat for all the leaves, cutting 3 or 4 fronds into the smallest leaf, 4 or 5 fronds into the 2½″ leaf, 5 or 6 fronds into the 3' leaf, and 6 or 7 fronds into the largest leaf. **F-G**

5. Add glue to the back seam of each leaf and insert a 6″ piece of 20-gauge floral wire. Nestle the wire tightly to the centerline so it's as straight as possible. Then fold over the flap and press down tightly to seal the wire inside the back of the leaf. Repeat for all 9 fronds. **H-I**

6. Lay out a parchment paper work surface. Using the pastel brush, add details to each leaf with both shades of PanPastel. Concentrate darker shades of pastel on the center of the fern, and then gently blend the lighter green tones on the fronds. **J**

7. Brush a light layer of Mod Podge onto both sides of each leaf with the foam brush. Brush with the paper grain. Let dry completely. **K**

F

G

H

I

J

K

ASSEMBLY

1. Align the smallest fern with the top of the 18″ wire—the main stem. Use the Grass Green assembly strips, dotted with glue, to tightly wrap the 2 stems together and attach them. Wrap until smooth. **A**

2. Move 1″ down the stem. Align the 2 leaves measuring 2½″ with the main stem, on opposite sides but even with one another. Wrap the stems tightly with the assembly strips, attaching them securely and smoothly to the main stem. **B-C**

3. Repeat Step 2 to add 2 of the 3″ leaves 1½″ down the main stem. **D**

4. Repeat Step 2 to add the 3½″ leaves 2″ down the main stem. **E**

5. Repeat Step 2 to add the final 2 leaves measuring 3″ down the main stem 2″. Wrap to the bottom of the main stem, completely covering it. **F**

A

B

C

D

E

F

MATERIALS

18-gauge cloth-covered floral wire

    3 pieces 18″

20-gauge paper-
covered floral wire

    18 pieces 5″

180-gram Italian crepe paper
in #568 (Cartotecnica Rossi)

160-gram German crepe paper
in Grass Green, Dark Green,
Red, and Sun Yellow (Werola)

PanPastel in Orange
and Permanent Red

Pastel brush

Mod Podge, matte

Foam brush

Curling tool (recommendation:
bead reamer)

Tacky glue

Scissors

Parchment paper

Templates Needed

Basic Leaf Template (page 175)

Maple Leaf Template (page 175)

PAPER CUTTING

Cut Assembly Strips (page 20) of:

    #568

      Dark Green

      Grass Green

Foliage

For many, foliage is often the most forgotten and least fun part of paper flower making. But it's one of my favorite things to make. It does wonders for a bouquet— adding texture and movement to an arrangement. The foliage in this chapter includes basic ideas that can be expanded and built upon as a framework for foliage and filler. There are three different example types of foliage in this chapter. The instructions and listed materials will make one of each foliage type.

Filler Leaves

Filler leaves are the easiest way to create texture and take up space in a bouquet. Vary the cutting patterns—thin fringe, thick fringe, skinny triangles, wide triangles—to make a variety of realistic and lively green stems. There are no templates for this style of foliage.

1. Cut 2 strips 3″ × 12″ of stretched out Grass Green.

2. Cut a pattern into each strip. Use the same pattern for each strip, but feel free to use whatever cutting pattern you prefer. Cut two-thirds of the way down the strip, leaving the bottom one-third untouched. I chose to use a medium-size triangle fringe pattern. **A-B**

3. Use the curling tool to curl the top edges of the fringe across the whole strip.**C**

4. Add a thin line of glue down the bottom edge of 1 strip. Wrap the strip carefully and evenly down a piece of the 18-gauge wire, starting at the top. The fringe should curl out, away from the stem. Don't let the fringe bunch up or leave any part of the stem bare. Use the second strip when the first strip ends. Choose where you want the wrap to stop—between two-thirds of the way down and the bottom of the wire. **D**

5. After you've stopped wrapping the fringe, use an assembly strip of Grass Green to wrap from where the foliage strip ends to the bottom of the wire. **E-F**

A

B

C

D

E

F

Autumnal Branch

Each autumnal branch has nine leaves.

1. Make 9 leaves from the Sun Yellow paper, following the instructions in Basic Leaves (page 20). Start with 3″ squares. Use the Basic Leaf template. **A**

2. Add glue to the back seam of each leaf and insert a 5″ piece of 20-gauge wire. Nestle the wire tightly to the centerline so it's as straight as possible. Then fold over the flap and press down tightly to seal the wire inside the back of the leaf. Repeat for all 9 leaves. **B-C**

3. Set up a parchment paper work surface. Use the pastel brush and the Permanent Red PanPastel to add details to each leaf (see Color, page 16). Add as much pigment as you desire, and vary the look slightly between each leaf. **D**

4. Brush a light layer of Mod Podge on the front and back of each leaf using the foam brush. Let dry completely. **E**

5. Cut a notched pattern all around the edges of each leaf, cutting at an angle with the paper grain. **F**

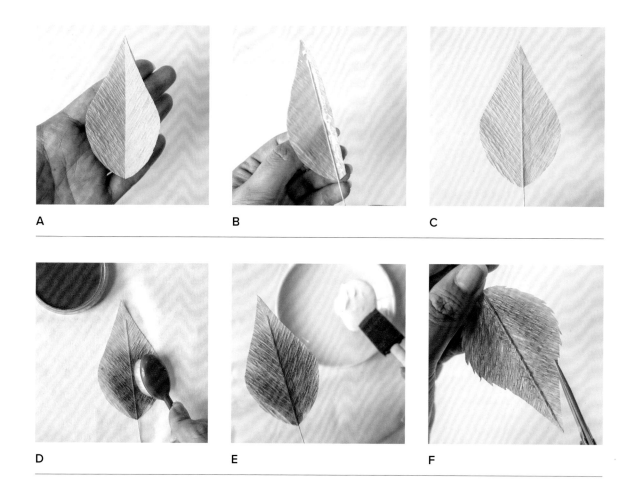

A

B

C

D

E

F

6. Dot the #568 assembly strips with glue, and then use them to wrap the leaf stems completely, starting at the base of each leaf and covering the wire. **G**

7. Lay 1 leaf flush with the top of the 18″ wire; then wrap tightly with strips from Step 6 to attach the 2 stems together. **H**

8. Add the next 8 leaves to the branch using the same wrapping method as Step 7. Place them about 1″ apart, alternating which side of the main branch you attach each leaf to and slightly curving each leaf stem. Vary the distance slightly, leaving a wider gap sometimes, for a more realistic branch. Wrap each leaf tightly and smoothly. Continue wrapping to the bottom of the stem after attaching the final leaf. **I**

9. Bend the main stem as shown for a more realistic branch. **J**

G   H   I   J

Maple Branch Variation

To make a Maple Branch, follow Steps 1–9 for the Autumnal Branch, using the following variations:

- Use the Maple Leaf template instead of the Basic Leaf template.

- Use Red crepe paper.

- Add PanPastel details with Orange.

ADDITIONAL FOLIAGE VARIATIONS • The Autumnal Branch is a great base for all kinds of foliage. You can use any leaf shape, paper color, and detailing with Steps 1–9 to create unique, specific, or customized leaf branches. The templates also include one Bonus Foliage Leaf template.

Projects

These projects use the florals and greenery from the previous section to make stunning pieces of home decor. As instructed, refer back to the chapter for each flower or plant to make the individual elements needed for each project.

Golden Ginkgo Wreath

Gingko leaves are striking in their own right, but in gold? Even more so.
This is also a great introduction to the magic of metallic crepe paper. It is truly spectacular. Feel free to
adjust the floral hoop size to make a series of different-size ginkgo wreaths to hang on your wall.

MATERIALS

6″ floral hoop (from Michaels or another craft supply store)

Tacky glue

Scissors

For 20 Ginkgo Leaves* (page 56):

    180-gram Italian crepe paper in #810 (Cartotecnica Rossi)

*See Notes on Materials below.

PAPER CUTTING

Cut Assembly Strips (page 20) of:

    #810

Notes on Materials

This wreath requires 20 complete Gingko leaves made from the #810 paper. Follow Steps 1–6 in Leaves (page 57). Make sure to consistently use the gold side of the paper for the front of each leaf.

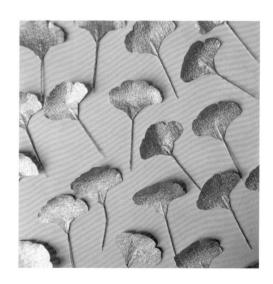

Assembly

1. Add glue to the #810 assembly strips. Use them to wrap the hoop completely. This can be a bit awkward, so use shorter length strips to make it easier. **A**

2. Using the assembly strips, combine all the ginkgo leaves into pairs, wrapping their wires together. Then curve the leaves in opposite directions. **B**

3. Use additional gold assembly strips to wrap the ginkgo pairs to the hoop. Lay the wires flush with the hoop; then wrap with the glued strips until smooth and secure. Add pairs all around the hoop. I placed my leaves evenly, all facing the same direction, but feel free to experiment with placement. Try adding them more densely in 1 area or bending the leaves in varying directions. **C-D**

A

B

C

D

Floral Wreath

Floral wreaths are timeless decor. They can be adjusted for the appropriate season and allow a great deal of creative license on the maker's part. In this example, I'm using complementary colors of blue and yellow with dark green leaves. There are no wrong colors or flowers so feel free to adjust to your personal taste. Like the gingko wreath, you can explore a variety of sizes, from the small and delicate to the big and bold. These not only make for beautiful decor, but also serve as thoughtful gifts.

MATERIALS

6″ floral hoop (from Michaels or another craft supply store)

Green floral tape

Mod Podge, matte

Foam brush

Tacky glue

Scissors

3 Butterfly Ranunculus*

10 Tweedia Flowers*

For 5 Autumnal Branch Variations*:

    German doublette paper in Leaf/Moss (Werola)

See Notes on Materials below.

Notes on Materials

This wreath requires three complete butterfly ranunculus flowers. Follow the instructions in Butterfly Ranunculus (page 114) to make each ranunculus on an 8″ stem, with no leaves or buds.

This wreath requires ten complete tweedia flowers. Follow Steps 1–16 in Flowers and Sepals (page 109) to make ten flowers with sepals. Do not include any buds or leaves. Wrap the flowers together in small bunches of two or three blooms with assembly strips (page 20) of Grass Green.

This wreath requires five complete leaf branches made from Leaf/Moss doublette paper. Each branch should have seven leaves. Follow the instructions in Autumnal Branch (page 152), but skip the PanPastel details and notches.

Assembly

1. Activate the floral tape by stretching it. Use it to wrap the first leaf branch to the floral hoop. Lay the bottom of the branch wire flush with the hoop, and wrap smoothly and securely. Each element will be added along the wire, overlapping the previous piece. **A**

2. Repeat Step 1 to add a butterfly ranunculus at the base of the first leaf branch. Add a second leaf branch next, sandwiching the ranunculus. Add 4 to 6 tweedia (2 bunches) on top of the second leaf branch. **B**

3. Add a third leaf branch, the second butterfly ranunculus, and the fourth leaf branch, again sandwiching the flower. Finish the hoop with the rest of the tweedia bunches, the final leaf branch, and the third ranunculus. **C-D**

A

B

C

D Back of hoop

Geranium Potted Plant

Some particular flower varieties look best displayed in a pot. Geraniums are one of these varieties. Daffodils and hyacinth would also be other types you could display in this format. The touch of preserved moss adds another level of realism to your flower. These pots are perfect for housewarming presents or for those of us whose green thumbs are a bit lacking.

MATERIALS

6″ terra-cotta flower pot

Flower pin frog (from Michaels or another craft supply store)

Dried moss (from Michaels or another craft supply store)

1 Geranium* (page 24)

See Notes on Materials below.

Notes on Materials

This potted plant requires a minimum of one geranium, but depending on the size of your pot, you may want to add multiple stems. Follow all the instructions in Geranium (page 24) to make one complete flower stem with leaves.

Assembly

1. Place the flower pin frog in the bottom of the pot. **A**

2. Fill the pot with the dried moss. **B**

3. Slide the geranium stem through the moss and secure it into the flower pin. If adding more than one geranium stem, cut the floral wire of some of the main stems so that they're not all at the same height. Adjust the moss if needed. **C-D**

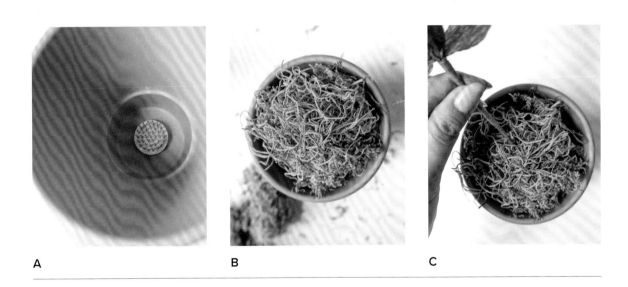

A   B   C

D

Autumnal Garland

There are few things more beloved than fall foliage. Even though the days may be growing shorter, the trade-off of all the yellow, orange, and red leaves makes it almost worth the loss of daylight. In this project, you'll create your own autumn leaves and transform them into the perfect garland for your holiday table, entryway, or staircase. This creates a 24˝ garland.

MATERIALS

18-gauge Kraft-paper-covered floral wire

3 pieces 18˝

160-gram German paper in Red, Orange, Terracotta, Forest Green, and Goldenrod (Werola)

Brown floral tape

PanPastel in Permanent Red, Bright Yellow Green, Hansa Yellow, Chrome Oxide Green, and Permanent Red Extra Dark

Pastel brush

Mod Podge, matte

Foam brush

Parchment paper

Leaf Preparation

This garland requires 45 to 50 finished leaves on wired stems. I suggest making an equal number of each leaf color, and varying each leaf slightly for a more realistic look.

Mix and match the paper colors and templates. I recommend using the Basic Leaf template (page 23), the Maple Leaf template (page 23), and the Geranium Leaf template (page 23), as well as freehand-cutting leaf shapes.

For all leaves, follow the instructions in Basic Leaves (page 20), starting with 4–6˝ squares. Then detail the leaves with PanPastel and coat both sides with a thin layer of Mod Podge. Finally, to wire each leaf, add glue to the back seam of each leaf and insert a 4˝ piece of 20-gauge wire. Nestle the wire tightly to the centerline so it's as straight as possible. Then fold over the flap and press down tightly to seal the wire inside the back of the leaf.

Assembly

1. Stretch the brown floral tape to activate it. Completely wrap the 18″ pieces of floral wire. **A**

2. Lay 2 of the 18″ wires flush with one another, overlapping by half. Wrap the 2 wires with the floral tape, continuing until smooth. Repeat, adding the third 18″ wire to the end of the new, longer wire. This new unit, approximately 36″ long, is the garland base.

3. Using the floral tape, add the leaves to the garland base one by one. Align the leaf wire; then wrap it to the main base. The placement pattern is: left side of the garland, right side of the garland, center of the garland. Use a varied assortment of leaves. **B-C**

4. Repeat this pattern down the entire length of the garland. Vary the placement slightly and the space between groupings, as desired. I placed each group close together, overlapping the leaves. Position and bend the leaves as desired once they have all been attached. **D-F**

5. Turn over the garland; then slightly bend and curve the garland base for a more realistic "branch" look. **G**

A   B   C   D

E

F

G

Monochromatic
Hand-Tied Bouquet

One of my favorite types of floral arrangements are monochrome-colored bouquets. Making a monochrome bouquet from paper flowers offers even more creative possibilities than real flowers, as you can truly choose the colors of each petal to match perfectly. You can even take this further than I do in this project, making matching color stems and leaves if you prefer. Though I'm using pink, choose any color you wish.

MATERIALS

Chicken wire (2mm thickness)

Wire cutter

Ribbon or string

2 pink peonies (see below)

2 pink butterfly ranunculus (see below)

3 pink Icelandic poppies (see below))

3 pink tulips (see right)

2 pink ranunculus (see right)

3 pink zinnias (see right)

2 pink dahlias (see right)

Individual Flower Preparation

Each flower should be created by following the instructions in the specific chapter noted, but with the variations indicated:

Make 2 pink peonies (page 88), each on an 18″ stem. Omit the leaves.

Make 2 pink butterfly ranunculus (page 114), each on an 18″ stem.

Make 3 pink Icelandic poppies (page 82), each on an 18″ stem. Vary the pinks used for more visual interest. I suggest starting with blush 48-gram paper for the petals, colored with Magenta PanPastel. Additional paper color options are #384, #390, or #391.

Make 3 pink tulips (page 102), each on an 18″ stem. Use 90-gram paper in #350 for the petals, and paint them as directed with Fluorescent Magenta acrylic paint (Golden) and Dr. Ph Martin's Cyclamen. Vary the saturation of the shades of pink for more variety. Include the leaves.

Make 2 pink ranunculus (page 122) in slightly different shades, each on an 18″ stem. Choose from the following doublette options: Light Rose/Pink, Peach/Pink, and Strawberry/Fraise for the petals. Omit the leaves and bud.

Make 3 zinnias (page 30), each on an 18″ stem. Choose from the following doublette options: Light Rose/Pink, Peach/Pink, Strawberry/Fraise, Blush/Chiffon, and Pink/Berry. Omit the leaves.

Make 2 dahlias (page 130), each on an 18″ stem. Choose from the following doublette options: Blush/Chiffon, Peach/Pink, or Light Rose/Pink. Color with Magenta PanPastel. Omit the leaves.

Assembly

1. Using wire cutters, cut a 12″ × 5″ piece of chicken wire. Fold the wire in half lengthwise to be a 6″ × 5″ rectangle. Gently mold the edges of the wire into an oval shape. **A**

2. Prepare to build the bouquet in your hand or on your working surface. Add each stem by threading it through the chicken wire. In the beginning, the stems may feel a bit loose and unstable, but the more stems you add, the more stable the bouquet will be.

Start by holding together some of the focal flowers—the large, showstopping blooms. Start with the dahlias, peonies, tulips, and butterfly ranunculi. They should be arranged so they don't appear symmetrical. Vary the heights and angles of the flowers. Hold the bouquet away from you to see how it is coming together from all sides, and adjust as needed.

3. Wrap the chicken wire from Step 1 around the middle of the stems. It should be tight enough to hold the flowers together, but loose enough that more blooms can still be added. **B**

4. Add more flowers—the zinnias, Icelandic poppies, and ranunculi. Arrange them between the focal flowers, complementing them. Fill in the gaps. Adjust the chicken wire if needed. **C**

A

B

C

5. Look at the bouquet from all sides. Adjust the arrangement, varying the heights of the flowers. Remove flowers if things look too crowded, or add more blooms if you have large gaps. Sometimes readjusting, bending, or swapping flowers can fix empty spaces.

6. Once you've finished adding the flowers, trim any excess stem length (if necessary). Very carefully, press the chicken wire tightly around the stem bases so the sharp ends are no longer pointing outward. Then use a ribbon of your choice to wrap around the chicken wire, covering it. Tuck the ribbon tightly underneath itself to secure it. **D-F**

D   E   F

Dutch Still-Life Arrangement

Dutch still lifes are my favorite paintings. Not only are the colors and subjects beguiling, but they provide a snapshot into life in a very different time and space. If you're not familiar with this style of painting, I highly recommend the artists Jan Davidsz. de Heem and Rachel Ruysch for inspiration.

Tulips are the most ubiquitous flowers in these paintings. They're often placed in unique ways, with the petals exposed and wilting low over the table or vase. I love that the artists show these flowers in an imperfect state. In general, the flowers in these paintings are not expertly placed—it's a bit messy but still beautiful.

MATERIALS

Compote bowl base

Floral frog (Funky Rock Design)

Wire cutter

Preserved moss (from Michaels or another craft supply store)

3 tulips (page 102)

3 Icelandic poppies (page 82)

3 tweedia (page 108)

1 English garden rose (page 72)

3 daffodils (page 38)

INDIVIDUAL FLOWER PREPARATION

For all flowers, make the flower as directed in each individual project, including leaves and buds as directed with one exception: make the English garden rose without leaves. Feel free to use different colors for the flowers.

Assembly

1. Place the flower frogs in the center of the compote bowl. Depending on the width of your compote bowl, you may need multiple frogs. I don't use floral pins; instead, I prefer to use stone floral frogs for their stability and variation. **A**

2. Add 2 tweedia, 3 daffodils, and 3 tulips into the frogs. Position them at different angles, crisscrossing around the bowl and creating a wide, far-reaching start to the bouquet. **B**

3. Then add the focal flowers—the Icelandic poppies and English garden rose. Place them around the vase, bending and shaping the stems as needed. To add more variation and texture, adjust the tulip petals so some are more open and some are more closed. They should be arranged so they don't appear symmetrical. Vary the heights and angles of all the flowers. Add the final tweedia hanging over the lip of the bowl. **C**

4. Look at the bouquet from all sides. Adjust the arrangement as needed. Remove flowers if things look too crowded, or add more blooms if you feel like there is too much negative space. Personally, I think the negative space can enhance an arrangement, so don't be too quick to keep adding. Sometimes less is more.

5. Once the flowers are in place, cover the base fully with preserved moss. **D-E**

A

B

C

D

E

Mushroom Cloche

Although mushrooms are fungi, they are botanically adjacent and the perfect accompaniment to paper flowers. Here you'll learn how to create your own magical woodland scene encased in a glass cloche, forever frozen in time. Be as fanciful as you choose, or make it as realistic as possible. These mushrooms are modeled off the real-life mushroom Amanita muscaria.

MATERIALS

180-gram Italian crepe paper in #603 (Cartotecnica Rossi)

Spun cotton mushroom caps, 1½″ (Smile Mercantile)

Wooden dowels ⅛″ thick
1 piece 3″

Wooden disk, 1½″ diameter

Drill and ⅛″ drill bit

Acrylic paint in Red (Golden)

Paintbrush

Air-dry clay (Model Magic)

Gloss Medium (Golden)

Foam brush

Wood glue

Preserved moss (from Michaels or another craft supply store)

Glass cloche 3½″ × 4¾″

Curling tool (recommendation: bead reamer)

Tacky glue

Scissors

Tweezers

Hot glue gun and glue sticks

Optional: gold paint (Design Master)

PAPER CUTTING

Cut Assembly Strips (page 20) of:

#603

Preparation

1. Using the drill and ⅛″ drill bit, drill a hole in the center of the wooden disk. If using the optional gold paint, spray-paint the wood gold. **A**

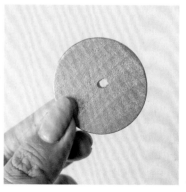

A

MUSHROOM

1. Add hot glue to the underside of the mushroom cap, over the precut hole, and insert the 3″ wooden dowel. **A**

2. Paint the top of the mushroom cap with the red paint. You will need to apply 2 or 3 coats. Take care to make sure all the nooks and crannies in the spun cotton have been painted. Let dry upright. **B-C**

3. Turn over the mushroom, and paint ¼″ under the mushroom cap. Let dry upright. **D**

4. Cover all the red areas in Gloss medium. Add additional layers to achieve a shinier finish. **E**

5. Mold small pieces of air-dry clay into 20 to 25 small circular shapes. They should not be uniform in size or shape. Let dry overnight. These are the scales for the cap. **F**

6. Using the tweezers, dip 1 scale into tacky glue, and then glue it to the red mushroom cap. There's no set pattern, so distribute them evenly around the cap, and only use the number you need to reach your desired look. **G-H**

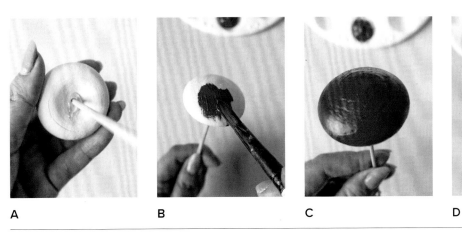

A   B   C   D

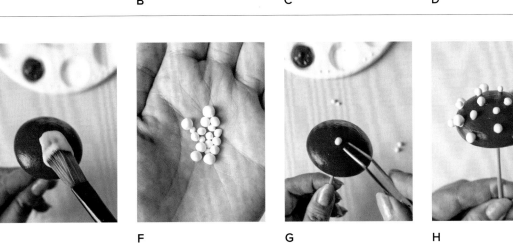

E   F   G   H

7. Cover the whole mushroom cap with a thin layer of gloss medium. **I**

8. If necessary, trim the dowel shorter so it will fit in the cloche.

9. Add glue to the #603 assembly strips, and wrap from the base of the mushroom cap until ½" from the bottom of the dowel. Decide how the stem will look—thin and skinny or thick and sturdy? Even and cylindrical or round and playful? Wrap back and forth up the stem until the desired stem thickness and shape are achieved. **J-K**

10. Cut a 1½‴ x 6" piece of #603, and stretch it as far as possible. Accordion-fold the strip into ¾" wide rectangles. Trim both folded edges, so you have a stack of individual rectangles. Fold each individual rectangle in half along 1 long side. Repeat to create 80 to 90 folded pieces. These are the gills for below the cap. **L-N**

I

J

K

L

M

N

11. Add a line of glue on the underside of the mushroom cap, running from the dowel to the red paint. Attach the fold of a gill to the line of glue using the tweezers or bead reamer to press it tightly to the cap. Repeat to attach gills around the entire underside of the cap. Start by adding 4 gills that divide the cap into quarters (think of a compass), and then fill in the space between them with tightly packed gills. Use the bead reamer to push gills into tight spaces. **O-R**

12. Trim the gills so they are even in length. They should be slightly longer than the edge of the mushroom cap. **S-T**

O

P

Q

R

S

T

13. Cut a ½″ × 1½″ piece of #603, making sure it has not been stretched. Use your fingertips to ruffle 1 long side of the rectangle, gently pulling the edge in opposite directions. Add a line of glue to the unruffled edge. **U**

14. Wrap the rectangle from Step 13 around the mushroom stem at any height. Then add more glue to the short side of the rectangle, pressing it together to create a ring around the stem. Press tightly, and then pull up the ruffled bottom edge so it stands away from the stem. Use a #603 assembly strip to wrap from the top of the ruffle rectangle to the base of the mushroom cap. Leave the bottom 1/2″ of the stem untouched. **V-X**

U   V   W   X

Assembly

1. Add a small amount of wood glue to the wooden dowel sticking out from the stem, and then insert the dowel into the wooden disk. **A**

2. Add wood glue to the center of the cloche base, and then glue the wooden disk and mushroom to the base. **B**

3. Place the preserved moss around the mushroom. Trim any excess that hangs over the edge of the cloche. Add the glass top to the cloche. **C-D**

A   B   C   D

Templates

All templates are provided in this section, and in a downloadable PDF. To access the template PDF, scan this QR code, or go to tinyurl.com/11575-patterns-download.

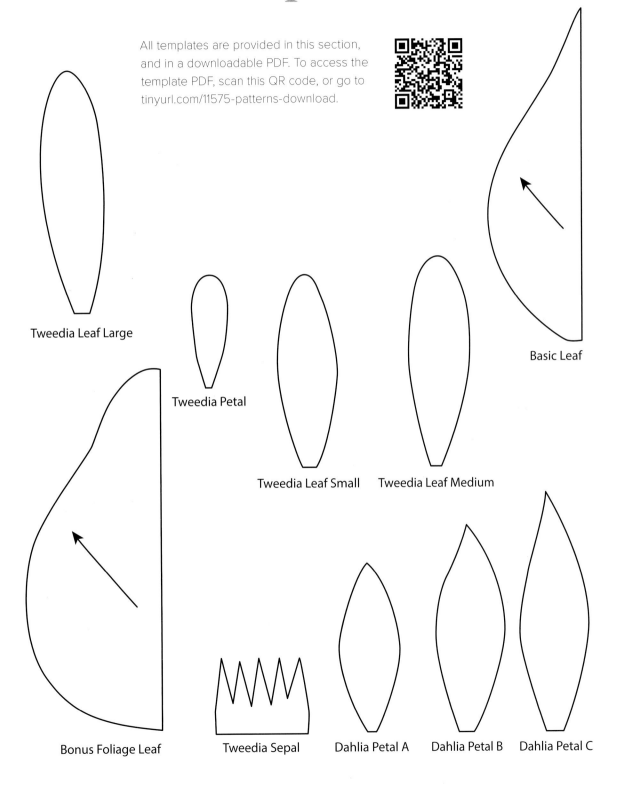

Tweedia Leaf Large

Basic Leaf

Tweedia Petal

Tweedia Leaf Small

Tweedia Leaf Medium

Bonus Foliage Leaf

Tweedia Sepal

Dahlia Petal A

Dahlia Petal B

Dahlia Petal C

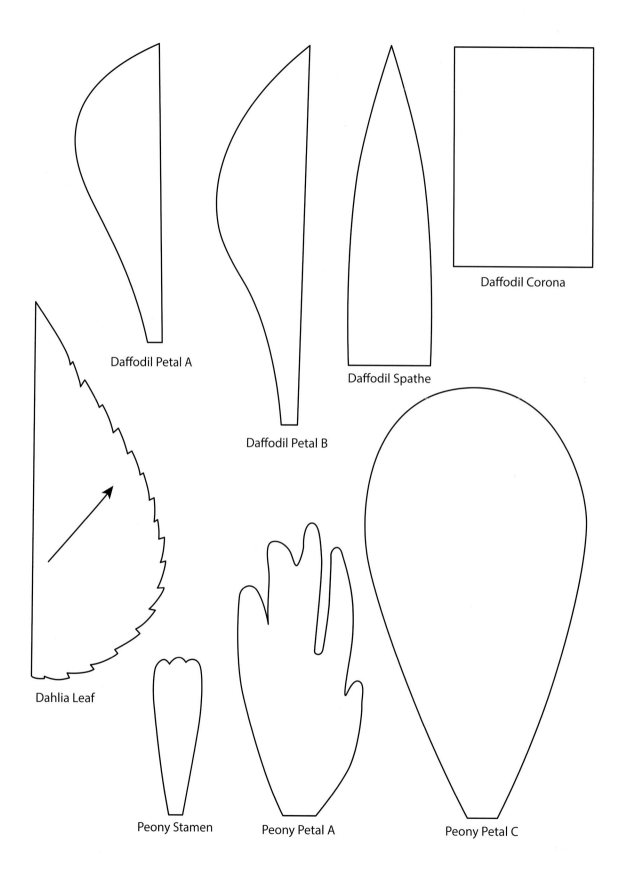

Daffodil Petal A

Daffodil Petal B

Daffodil Spathe

Daffodil Corona

Dahlia Leaf

Peony Stamen

Peony Petal A

Peony Petal C

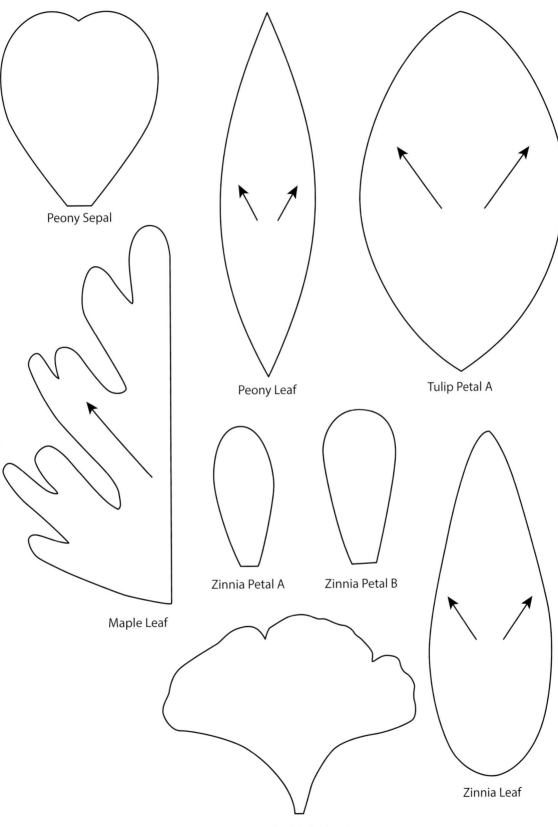

Peony Sepal

Peony Leaf

Tulip Petal A

Maple Leaf

Zinnia Petal A

Zinnia Petal B

Zinnia Leaf

Gingko Biloba Leaf

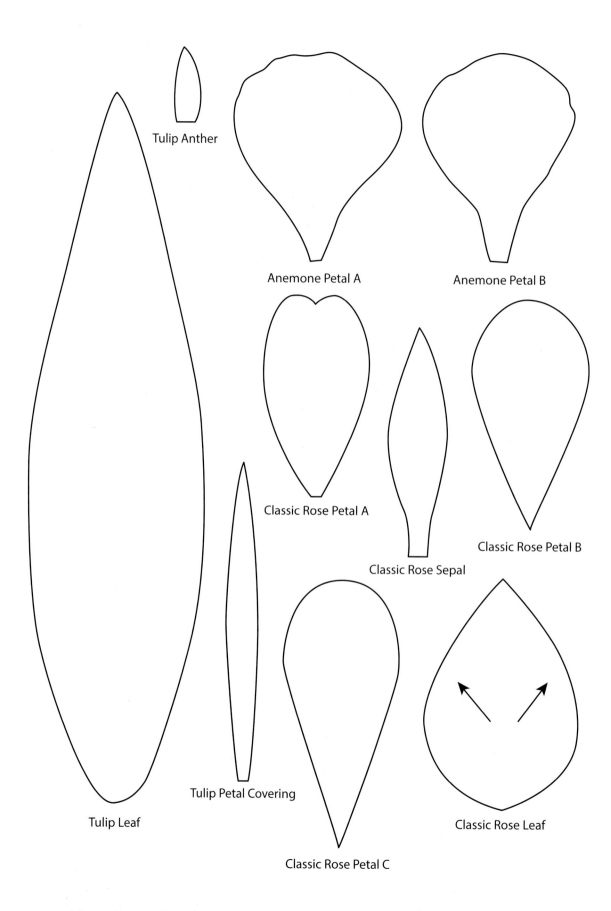

Tulip Anther

Anemone Petal A

Anemone Petal B

Classic Rose Petal A

Classic Rose Sepal

Classic Rose Petal B

Tulip Petal Covering

Tulip Leaf

Classic Rose Leaf

Classic Rose Petal C

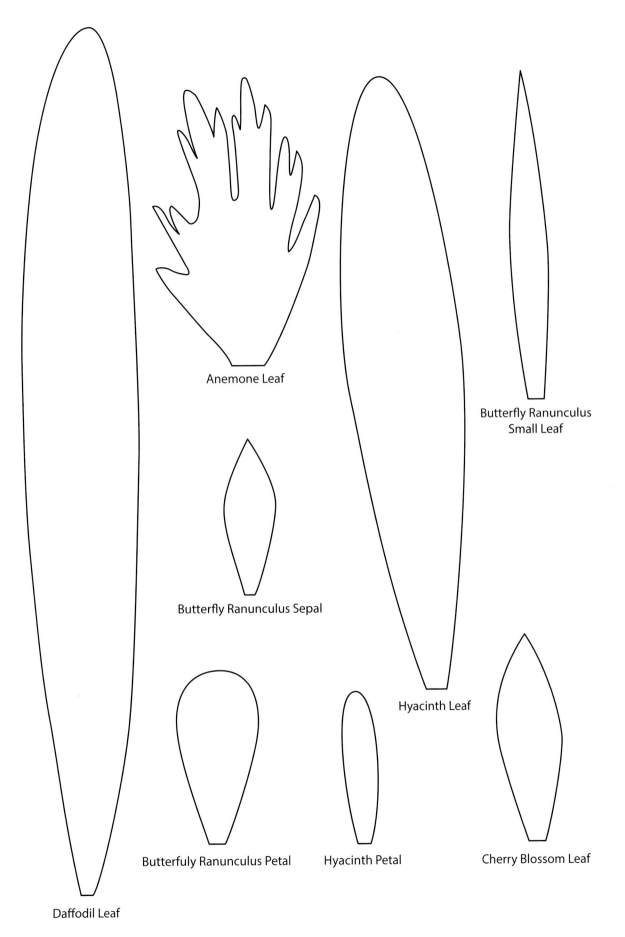

Anemone Leaf

Butterfly Ranunculus
Small Leaf

Butterfly Ranunculus Sepal

Hyacinth Leaf

Butterfuly Ranunculus Petal

Hyacinth Petal

Cherry Blossom Leaf

Daffodil Leaf

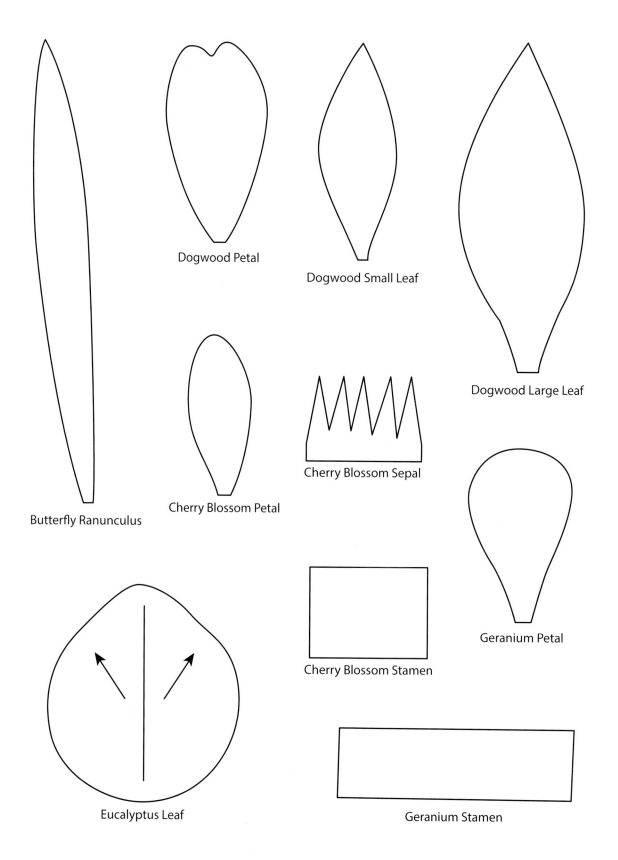

Dogwood Petal

Dogwood Small Leaf

Dogwood Large Leaf

Butterfly Ranunculus

Cherry Blossom Petal

Cherry Blossom Sepal

Geranium Petal

Eucalyptus Leaf

Cherry Blossom Stamen

Geranium Stamen

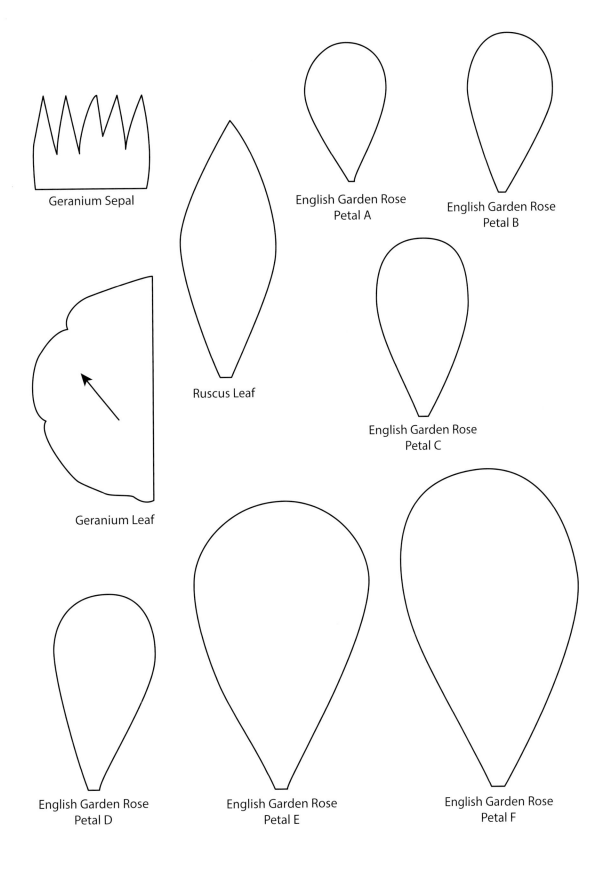

Geranium Sepal

Ruscus Leaf

English Garden Rose
Petal A

English Garden Rose
Petal B

Geranium Leaf

English Garden Rose
Petal C

English Garden Rose
Petal D

English Garden Rose
Petal E

English Garden Rose
Petal F

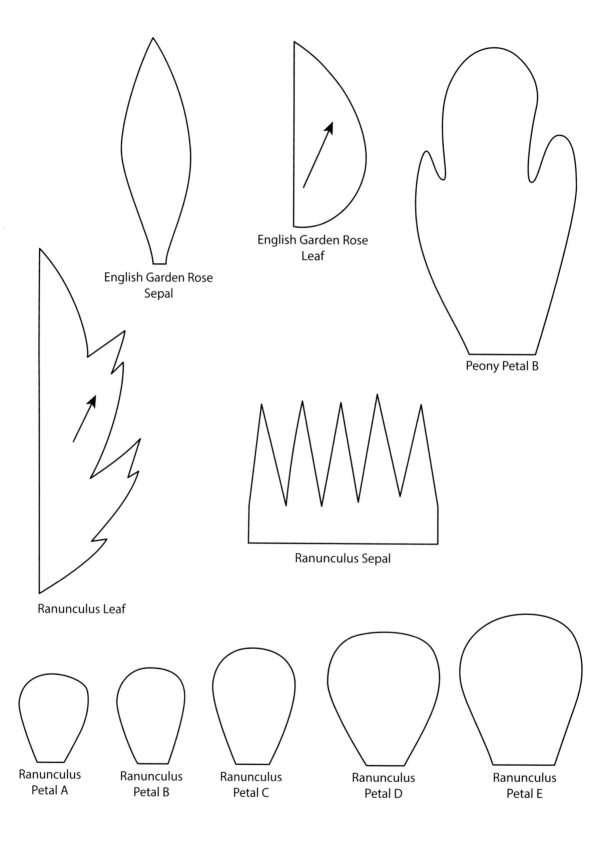

English Garden Rose
Sepal

English Garden Rose
Leaf

Peony Petal B

Ranunculus Leaf

Ranunculus Sepal

Ranunculus
Petal A

Ranunculus
Petal B

Ranunculus
Petal C

Ranunculus
Petal D

Ranunculus
Petal E

About the Author

Emily Paluska is a Korean American botanical artist. She has had the privilege of teaching students all around the world how to make paper flowers.

Her work has been displayed at the National Gallery of Art in Washington, D.C. She has also taught for the National Gallery of Art and the Smithsonian American Art Museum. Emily's work has been featured in *HGTV Magazine, Veranda*, at the National Cherry Blossom Festival, among a variety of other print and online publications. A career high for her was being asked to create part of the official gift to President Yoon Suk Yeol from President Joseph Biden, fully combining her Korean and American sides in one project.

Born in Busan, South Korea, Emily is now located in Washington, D.C., where you can find her making flowers or kimchi. Find her online at reverypaperflora.com or on all social media platforms @reverypaperflora.

CREATIVE SPARK
ONLINE LEARNING

Quilting courses to become an expert quilter...

From their studio to yours, Creative Spark instructors are teaching you how to create and become a master of your craft. So not only do you get a look inside their creative space, you also get to be a part of engaging courses that would typically be a one or multi-day workshop from the comfort of your home.

Creative Spark is not your one-size-fits-all online learning experience. We welcome you to be who you are, share, create, and belong.

Scan for a gift from us!

creativespark.ctpub.com